THE
SOVIET
UNION
The World's Largest Country

by John Gillies

Dillon Press, Inc. Minneapolis, Minnesota 55415

Photographs courtesy of the following: Associated Press/ Wide World—56, 58, 59, 64, 65, 140; ©Carrie Boretz/Archive—12, 38, 40, 91, 99, 101, 114, 118; L. Wayne Bryan—14, 89, 94, 112; Karl Dolgener—78; John Gillies—8, 18, 52; ©Lori Grinker/Archive—80, 104, 129; Intourist, the U.S.S.R. Company for Foreign Travel—16, 26, 33, 45, 48, 72, 88; Rose Lancaster—84, 116, 124; National Symphony/Jack Buxbaum—144; United Nations—22, 68, 111; UPI/ Bettman Archive—126, 131, 146. Cover photo: May Day parade by L. Wayne Bryan. Photo, page 8, St. Basil's Church in Red Square, Moscow.

Library of Congress Cataloging in Publication Data

Gillies, John, 1925-
   The Soviet Union : the world's largest country.

   Includes index.
   Summary: Discusses the geography, history, economy, family and school life, customs, and other aspects of life in the Soviet Union and examines the experiences of Soviet emigrants in the United States.
      1. Soviet Union—Juvenile literature.   [1. Soviet Union]   I. Title.
DK17.G55   1985   947   84-23024
ISBN 0-87518-290-9

Dillon Press, Inc., 242 Portland Avenue South
Minneapolis, Minnesota 55415

Printed in the United States of America
        4 5 6 7 8 9 10 93 92 91 90 89 88

Contents

Fast Facts About the Soviet Union

Official Name: *Soyuz Sovyetskikh Sotsialisticheskikh Respublik* (Union of Soviet Socialist Republics)

Capital: Moscow

Location: The Soviet Union covers one-half of Europe and one-third of Asia. To its north is the Arctic Ocean; to the east, Poland, Czechoslovakia, Hungary, and Romania; to the south, Turkey, Iran, Afghanistan, and China; its western border is the Bering Sea and the Sea of Okhotsk.

Area: 8,649,500 square miles (22,401,200 square kilometers); from east to west, its greatest distance is 6,800 miles (10,994 kilometers), and from north to south it is 3,200 miles (5,150 kilometers). The Soviet Union has 30,878 miles (49,547 kilometers) of coastline.

Elevation: *Highest*—Communism Peak, 24,590 feet (7,495 meters) above sea level. *Lowest*—the Karagiye Depression, 433 feet (132 meters) below sea level.

Population: Estimated population for 1984—274,992,000. *Distribution*—68 percent of the people live in or near cities; 32 percent live in rural areas. *Density*—31 persons per square mile (12 per square kilometer).

Form of Government: Socialist republic (Communist dictatorship).

Some Important Products: Barley, corn, cotton, oats, potatoes; beef cattle, dairy cattle, sheep; chemicals, electrical products, iron and steel, lumber; bauxite, coal, copper, iron ore, petroleum; transportation equipment, machinery.

Basic Unit of Money: Ruble.

Major Language: Russian.

Major Religions: The Soviet government encourages atheism, the belief that there is no God. Many Soviet citizens are members of the Russian Orthodox Church, while others might be Jewish, Muslim, or a member of another Christian church.

Flag: The Soviet flag is red, which stands for revolution. The upper left corner has three elements in gold: a hammer, representing workers; a sickle, representing farmers; and a star, representing the Communist Party.

National Anthem: "Gosudarstveny Gimn Sovetskogo Soyusa" ("National Anthem of the Soviet Union").

Major Holidays: Great October Revolution Day—November 7; May Day—May 1; VE Day—May 9; New Year's Day—January 1.

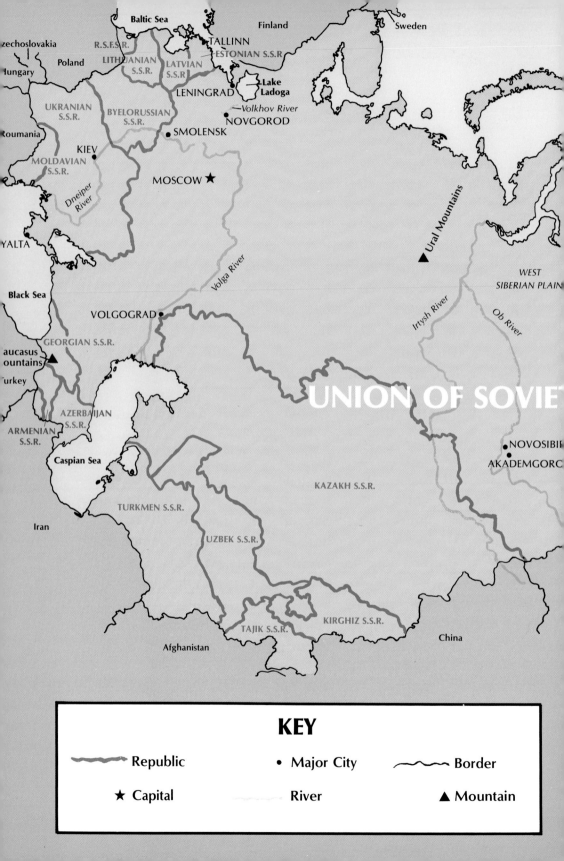

KEY

〰️ Republic   • Major City   〰️ Border

★ Capital   〰️ River   ▲ Mountain

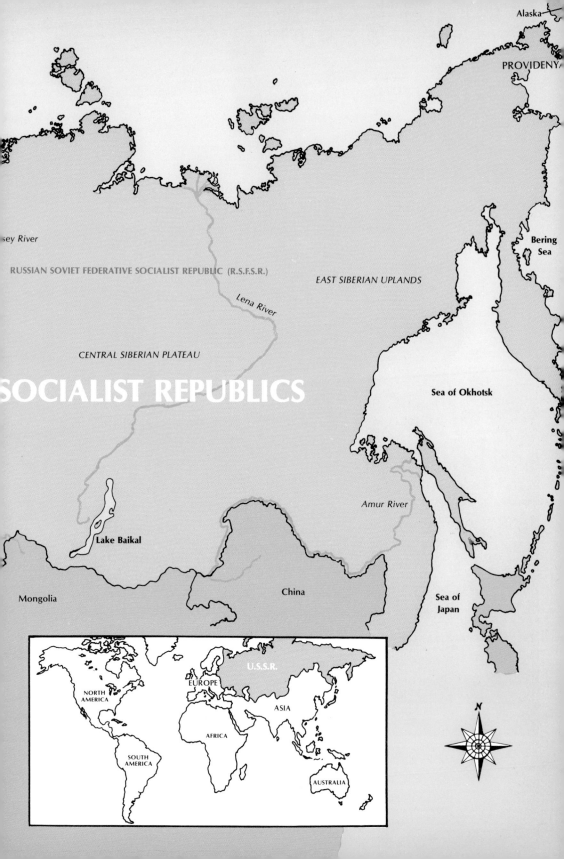

Alaska

PROVIDENYA

sey River

RUSSIAN SOVIET FEDERATIVE SOCIALIST REPUBLIC (R.S.F.S.R.)

EAST SIBERIAN UPLANDS

Lena River

Bering
Sea

CENTRAL SIBERIAN PLATEAU

SOCIALIST REPUBLICS

Sea of Okhotsk

Lake Baikal

Amur River

Mongolia

China

Sea of
Japan

NORTH
AMERICA

EUROPE

U.S.S.R.

ASIA

AFRICA

SOUTH
AMERICA

AUSTRALIA

N

1. Mother Russia

The largest country on earth: most people call it Russia. Its official name, however, is the Union of Soviet Socialist Republics, and the short form of that name is the U.S.S.R. Sometimes it's called the Soviet Union. But Mother Russia is what its people affectionately call it.

It is not just big; it is huge. If you had the energy (and the permission!) to walk around the entire Soviet Union in a circle, you would have to walk 37,000 miles, or 60,000 kilometers.

Let's say an Estonian student is finishing breakfast in Tallinn, getting ready to go to school. Tallinn is near the Baltic Sea, just across from Sweden. At the same time, one of her friends, in Providenya, just across from Alaska, would be putting away the supper dishes and getting ready to do some homework. To visit her friend, the Estonian student would have to cross eleven different time zones. This means she would have to move her watch one hour ahead eleven different times.

The Soviet Union is two-and-a-half times the size of the United States. It covers one-sixth of the earth's land surface. Beginning in the west at the Baltic Sea, the Soviet Union stretches over six thousand miles eastward to the Sea of Japan and the Bering Sea. The Arctic Ocean surrounds its northern frontier. The Soviet Union's southern border touches two other large bodies of water: the Black Sea and the Caspian Sea. That border also touches Turkey, Iran, Afghanistan, and China. Its western frontier touches Romania, Hungary, Poland, and Finland. (That's a big difference from the United States, with its neighbors.)

Have you ever heard the "Song of the Volga Boatmen?" The Volga is the largest river in Europe. It's nearly 2,200 miles long, and flows into the Caspian Sea. There are seven hydroelectric power plants on this river, the biggest one just outside Volgograd whose twenty-two generators produce eleven-and-a-half billion kilowatt-hours of electricity each year. And there are still "Volga boatmen," not only on the river, but also on the dammed-up lakes on the Volga used for recreation. Today they pull barges or pilot speedy hovercraft vessels and large cruise ships.

Many Soviet rivers are larger than our Mississippi. The Ob-Irtysh is a thousand miles longer. The Lena, which flows northward into the Arctic Ocean, is four hundred miles longer. Other challengers to the Mississippi are the Yenisey and the Amur rivers.

Rivers aren't the only large bodies of water. Lake Baikal in Siberia, at more than a mile deep, is the deepest lake in the world. That one lake contains one-fifth of the entire world's supply of fresh water.

The Soviet Union is also large because of its many people. Its population is approaching the three hundred million mark. More than one hundred different languages are spoken, although Russian is the common official language.

Sometimes it's hard to know whether you are in Europe or Asia, because the Soviet Union occupies parts of both continents: one-half of Europe and one-third of Asia. This is why so many languages are spoken and why there are so many different kinds of people.

What Is the U.S.S.R.?

In the Russian alphabet, U.S.S.R. is spelled CCCP, which would actually be "SSSR" in our alphabet. That first "S" stands for *Soyuz*, which is the Russian word for "union." You may have heard the word *Soyuz* as the name of a Soviet space ship. It is a Soviet *Union* because a group of states was formed in 1922, which has grown now to fifteen republics (or states). The peoples of these republics are often very different from one another. You will see blond-haired children in Estonia and dark-haired children in Armenia. Some wear fur hats like the ones you've seen in pictures of

Soviet children have various ethnic backgrounds.

Genghis Khan. Some children look Chinese. Some look like Eskimos.

The second "S" is for *Soviet*, which means "council." At the beginning of the 1900s, when the Russian people rebelled against their *czar*, or king, meetings or councils were held everywhere. There were councils in factories, on farms, in villages, and in cities. These were called soviets.

Socialist, the third "S", refers to the type of economy and government of the Soviet Union. Industry, communications, and transportation are owned by "society," by all of the people, not by individuals or even small groups of individuals. The English words *society* and *socialism* come from the same Latin word, *socius*; it means "partner." (Our English word *associate* also comes from that same root.) The Soviet Union is governed by the Communist Party, and Communism is an extreme form of socialism. Everything has a plan. "Planned enterprise" is the opposite of "free enterprise," which is the economic system of the United States.

The last word in the name of this country is *Republics*. Fifteen republics or states make up the Soviet Union, as already mentioned. That's somewhat like the fifty states that make up the United States. Each of the Soviet republics has its own legislature.

The Soviet flag is red, with a gold hammer and sickle placed below a gold-edged star, which is in its upper left corner. The hammer and sickle stand for the two groups that brought about the revolution against the czar in 1917. Factory workers are represented by the hammer. Farmers are represented by the sickle, which is a curved blade with a handle used to cut grain.

Red is a favorite color. You see it not only on the flag but as the background for huge banners and signs. The Red Star is a national symbol. It is put on the hats of soldiers and tops the towers of the Kremlin, in Moscow.

Red, a favorite color, is krasnaya *in Russian, meaning "beautiful." It is often used in decorations and signs. (The sign with the flowers on it says "Peace.)*

You've probably heard about the "Red" Army, but that doesn't have anything to do with the color of its uniforms, which are a dark green. Also, you've probably seen pictures on television of Red Square in Moscow, where there are important parades in May and November. It isn't red, either. You see, the Russian word for "red" is *krasnaya*, which also means "beautiful." Many Soviets think that this gigantic plaza outside the Kremlin is truly a "beautiful square."

Cities Old and New

Visitors to the Soviet Union could get a look at both the old and the new by visiting some of the larger cities. For instance, Kiev is called "the mother of Russian cities." Today it's the capital of the Ukrainian Soviet Socialist Republic, but once it was the capital of all Russia. Its history goes back to the tenth century. The Ukrainians, who make up most of Kiev's two-million population, are proud of their past and their language. The Ukrainian language is as different from Russian as Spanish is from Italian; there are some similarities, but they are two distinct languages.

Kiev straddles both banks of the Dnieper River. It is a transportation center for the Ukraine's many agricultural products. Also, there are rich deposits nearby of coal, iron ore, natural gas, and oil. This explains why Kiev has so many factories, which specialize in making heavy machinery. As a reflection of this, its huge sports center is called Dynamo Stadium, named for its famous Dynamo soccer team. (*Dynamo* is an old word for an electric generator.)

If you were asked to name the most important city in Russia, you would probably say Moscow. The Soviet Union's largest city, it is the capital of both the Russian Republic and the entire Soviet Union. Most news reports from the Soviet Union come out of Moscow.

Soviet ballet dancers are often called the world's best.

Moscow is the city Soviet citizens most like to visit. It is a center of government and education. Shopping is a popular activity here, and Moscow is an entertainment capital. Here is the famous Bolshoi ballet company, whose dancers and choreographers greatly influenced ballet today. The Moscow Circus is world famous; it travels all over the world. In the city are dozens of theatres, where people flock to see the latest plays. Most people would like to move to Moscow, but this requires special permission. Moscow already has eight million citizens.

Its first fortress, or *kremlin*, was begun in 1367, and because of destruction by invasions or fires has been rebuilt many times. Placed on a hill, in the shape of a triangle, the Kremlin walls surround many churches, palaces, an armory, towers, and other buildings. Soviet citizens visit the Kremlin to see the ancient treasures of the czars which are kept there. They also come to see Lenin's tomb (Lenin was the first leader of the Soviet Union). The ultra-modern, glass-and-aluminum Palace of the Congresses is also in the Kremlin.

The Kremlin also houses the twin towers of Ivan the Great, which are the tallest structures in Moscow. They contain a total of seventy-three bells, two of which weigh more than sixty tons. The Czar Bell, now at ground level, is the largest bell in the world. It is twenty feet high and weighs two hundred tons. Soviet families like to climb to the tops of the towers where they can see twenty miles in any direction.

They see the "new Moscow." Hotel Rossiya, just across Red Square, has three thousand rooms. Moscow has wide avenues and tall buildings. In the distance, on the Lenin Hills, they can see the Moscow University.

In Moscow, old and new buildings are often side by side. Since World War II, tall new buildings have been constructed, many of them apartment buildings.

Near the Kremlin is the Lenin State Library, which contains thirty million books. There are several reading rooms, where up to 2,500 people can read at tables at one time. Ten thousand people a day come to this library to read and to do research. Many come from remote places in the Soviet Union and spend their vacations reading. There are 400,000 libraries in the Soviet Union, including those in schools and factories, but the Lenin Library in Moscow has a copy of every book ever published in the country, historical documents and manuscripts, and many books published in the West, found nowhere else in the land.

When compared with Kiev and Moscow, Leningrad is a fairly new city. It was built by Czar Peter the Great in the early eighteenth century. First called St. Petersburg, its name was changed to Petrograd during World War I. After Lenin's death in 1924, the city was renamed Leningrad.

Peter built this city to be a "window" to the Western world. It is a port connected to the Bay of Finland, the Baltic Sea, and beyond. It is the most "European" of Russian cities. Some people think it looks like Paris because of its formal buildings and street lamps. Others think it looks like Amsterdam because of its many canals.

Because the czar once lived there, Leningrad has many palaces, churches, buildings, and monuments which reflect Russian history. The Leningrad Symphony is world class, and there is a ballet and opera company as well. The former Winter Palace of the czars now houses the world-famous Hermitage Museum, which is one of the truly great art galleries anywhere.

Leningrad has figured in more recent history as well. It was here that the revolution of 1917 began, with Lenin himself urging workers to revolt. Also, during World War II, the Nazis had Leningrad under attack for nearly three years. A third of Leningrad's population died—one million people in all—many from starvation. Getting enough food from across the salt marshes that border Leningrad is one of the great stories of wartime courage.

Novosibirsk (which means "new Siberia") is Siberia's largest city, with more than a million inhabitants, and it is still growing. Novosibirsk is the eighth largest city in the Soviet Union.

For centuries, Siberia was a place where Russian rulers exiled prisoners, who often died from cold and hard work. Today, it is the new frontier of the Soviet Union. It's an exciting place. Some people even call it the "wild east!" We often hear about Siberian "salt mines." There isn't any salt there, but oil, coal, and even diamonds are close by. Drilling and mining go on around the clock.

The city of Novosibirsk is young and fresh with modern buildings. Its streets form square blocks; there are no narrow, winding streets such as you find in older cities like Kiev.

Summers there are hot—up to 90 degrees Fahrenheit. That doesn't sound like Siberia! But wait—winter temperatures sometimes drop to 50 degrees below zero, with snow measured not by feet but by yards!

Novosibirsk is a transportation hub on the Trans-Siberian Railway, which was completed less than a hundred years ago. There's a school here that trains railway engineers. Railroads are a vital means of transportation in this big land. The civic theatre in Novosibirsk seats more people than the Bolshoi Theatre in Moscow. Its sports arena can hold 80,000. The city has its own ballet company, a circus, and a symphony orchestra. There are five hundred libraries.

And twenty miles to the south of Novosibirsk is a city called Akademgorodok, a sparkling new "science city" where 24,000 scientists are at work in twenty-two research centers.

That's modern Siberia!

The Soviet Countryside

But what is life like outside these large cities? One out of ten Soviet citizens lives in a village and most

Machinery and many hands are required to run a collective farm. Here farmers in Soviet Georgia use machines to pick tea leaves.

likely is a farmer. These farmers work on large *collective* farms. This means the farms and the food they produce are owned by the state, although the farmers may be permitted to plant a few vegetables near their homes.

The farmers live in villages, as farmers have done throughout Russian history. The average population of a village is just over two hundred people. Wooden houses called *izbas* are lined up on either side of a single street, which may be paved with cobblestones. There is a small school. And there may be a church if the village is Christian, a synagogue if Jewish, or a mosque if the villagers are Muslims.

The short summers are a busy time, when the farmers plant and harvest. The winters are long and cold. Farm families spend their time repairing tools, building furniture, weaving cloth, or watching TV.

The villages have electricity, and the state farms use modern tractors and other farm equipment. But villagers are often stuck where they are, due to the lack of paved roads. The roads are thick with mud in the spring and fall from melting snow or falling rain. In winter they are covered with snow so that even today the best way to travel is by horse and sleigh.

Soviet citizens everywhere like to tell you how beautiful their country is. There are lovely beaches along the Baltic and the Black seas. There is good skiing in the Caucasus, a mountain range that extends between the Black and Caspian seas. The highest mountain is called Communism Peak, 24,590 feet high, and is located near the China border. Close by is the lowest place in the Soviet Union, the Karagiye Depression, which is 433 feet below sea level. One-tenth of the country is desert, whose only inhabitants are wandering nomads. But even deserts can be beautiful in an uncluttered, quiet way. The flatlands, called the steppes, begin in the west in the Ukraine and stretch for hundreds of miles in all directions. Here are found some of the most fertile fields in all the world.

There is a six-thousand-mile-long birch and pine forest extending from Norway through northern Siberia to the Bering Sea. Except for the Ural Mountains, east of Moscow, which cut across the country almost vertically, all of the land across the Soviet Union is rather flat. The large mountains just mentioned are in the south or in central Asia.

Traveling Through the U.S.S.R.

About one-fourth of the Soviet Union is "off limits" to foreign travelers. It is said this is due to the lack of hotels. The reason may also be related to military activities. Even so, there is much to see that is not forbidden, and many ways to get there.

Aeroflot is the official (and only) airline allowed to operate inside the country, although a few foreign airlines do land in Moscow and Leningrad. Aeroflot has a large fleet of modern jet aircraft, designed by Soviet engineers and built within the Soviet Union. Once you are seated, the flight attendant doesn't talk about oxygen masks or exits. Instead, you'll hear that you are not allowed to smoke, to drink alcohol, to play a radio, or to take photographs.

There are many fine passenger trains. The most

famous of these is the Trans-Siberian Railroad, which takes eight days to cross five thousand miles. All of the trains west of Moscow run on electricity.

There are many new highways and frequent buses between cities. There are fewer private automobiles than in the United States, Canada, or Western Europe, but a small number of Soviet citizens do own cars. Most of these are made in the Soviet Union. Visitors are sometimes permitted to drive their own cars, but are restricted to certain routes and highways.

In the cities, there are electric trolleys and electric buses. There are no conductors on them. You buy a ticket at newsstands, and ride on a kind of "honor system." Occasionally an inspector may appear to ask to see your ticket. But normally you just board the bus or trolley, and when you leave you throw your paper ticket into a wastebasket.

Larger cities have subways. In Moscow, the subway trains stop every three minutes during rush hours. There, subway station walls are beautifully decorated with pictures and mosaics (pictures made with tiny pieces of stone). Some are even lit by fancy chandeliers, something you would expect to see in a great palace, not in a subway!

City streets and buildings are very clean. There are no graffiti, and there are heavy fines for littering. People are employed to keep the cities clean and attrac-

One of the most beautiful areas of the Soviet Union is the pine-and-birch forest in the north. This wooded area is home to many animals trapped for their fur.

tive; many of these are older women. One afternoon each week high school students are required to give their time trimming bushes or cleaning up parks. Elementary school children also have their own work days. In fact, every citizen is expected to help clean up and fix up at least one day a year, usually the third Saturday in April, called a shared-work day. Spring is a fine time for cleaning up, especially after the harsh winters that much of the Soviet Union endures.

Shortages and Problems

The Soviet Union has many resources—many raw materials, many factories and farms, and many workers. Nevertheless, it faces many shortages. Sometimes the shortages are because of bad weather or other natural conditions. Sometimes the problem comes from historic conditions, like war. Yet other problems arise from poor planning.

In spite of much good soil, there are shortages of food. Grain and meat have to be imported from the West, much of this from the United States and Canada. There is a shortage of consumer goods, things like children's shoes or refrigerators. The factories are told which products to manufacture, and this makes it harder to keep up with what people need and want. The Soviet Union tries to improve this situation by better

planning and by importing more manufactured things
from Hungary, East Germany, and its other allies.
There is also a shortage of housing. So many buildings
were destroyed during World War II that new construc-
tion doesn't keep up with demand. Most people con-
sider themselves lucky to have a two-room apartment.

There is a shortage of freedom, as it is known in the
West. You cannot easily change jobs. You cannot move
to another city until you first find a new job in that city.
You are not likely to get permission to take a vacation
outside of the country. Criticism of the government is
not allowed, although once in a while you will see a
letter to the editor in a paper complaining about slow
production in a factory or a poorly-made pair of shoes.
You cannot buy a newspaper or magazine that is published in the outside world. In this land of workers,
once called a "workers' paradise," workers are not
allowed to strike. The government is the employer, and
you don't strike against the government.

Serious problems exist between the East and the
West. The Soviet government says it is afraid of being
invaded. It has formed the Warsaw Pact with its allies
as a response to NATO (the North Atlantic Treaty
Organization), a U.S.-European military group. The
Soviet Union spends enormous amounts of money on
weapons. It sent its troops into Hungary and Czechoslovakia when people in those two countries rebelled

against their Communist governments. It still keeps large armies in Poland and East Germany. In Africa, Asia, Latin America, and the Middle East the Soviet Union has supplied weapons to revolutionary groups. It also invaded Afghanistan.

In turn, because Westerners do not understand why the Soviet Union goes beyond its borders, we also spend large sums on weapons. We say we want to be friends with the Soviet people, that they have nothing to fear from the West. We want to agree on limiting weapons on both sides. And we would like people to be able to choose freely on how and where they want to live. We believe we must keep on talking with each other.

The Soviet Union will be seventy years old in 1987. During that time, it has jumped from a land of horse-drawn plows to the nation that put the first cosmonaut in space.

It is important to learn more about this gigantic and fascinating country.

2. Patience, Pride, Patriotism

To more fully understand the Soviet people we also need to look at Soviet history. Over the years there have always been at least two classes of people: the *intelligentsia* (or, "the intelligent ones") and the *muzhiki* (or peasants).

The intelligentsia were the educated, wealthy, and high-born people. In the days of the czars, most of them were members of the nobility who preferred to speak French rather than Russian. In fact, they often seemed embarrassed to be Russians. Today's intelligentsia in the Communist system are engineers and scientists, who enjoy a higher standard of living than the average citizen. They have special privileges: They can shop at stores that carry hard-to-get items. They own cars and live in comfortable apartments. Sometimes they are allowed to have an *izba* (vacation home) in the country.

The second class of people, traditionally, has been the muzhiki. Once they were actually slaves, and were called *serfs*, a word from the Latin *servus*, which means "servant" or "slave." Although they could not read or write, they loved their land and their language. They were proud to speak Russian and to be Russian.

There are no serfs in modern Russia, and almost everyone knows how to read and write. Still, there are common people who have not gone beyond elementary school (or, at best, a vocational school) who are assigned to work on the land or in a factory for their entire lives.

Soviet Politics

Perhaps these divisions help explain why Soviet citizens are not "democratic" as this term is understood in the West. There are elections at least once every five years, but there is only one slate of candidates. You must be very brave to write in the name of some other person for whom you wish to vote. There are no referendums; there are no primaries to determine who will be the official candidates. Debates between candidates and political advertising do not exist. The Congress approves the selection of the president; the people do not vote for their top leaders.

The Soviet Union's Congress is called the *Supreme Soviet*. It has two "houses," the *Soviet of the Union* and the *Soviet of Nationalities*. Each has 750 members. The Congress approves budgets, and ratifies decrees and laws prepared at a higher level. The kind of political debate that is common in Western congresses is never heard here.

The Communist Party is the only political party. It had eighteen-and-a-half million members in 1985. The Soviet Constitution defines it as "the leading and guiding force in Soviet society." Its policies are approved by a "Congress of the Communist Party of the Soviet Union," with representatives from each of the fifteen republics.

These lawmaking groups follow the lead of the *Politburo*, which is something like an executive board or committee. It has fourteen official members, plus eight candidate members ("understudies" who could fill in if needed). The secretary of the Communist Party, the prime minister (or premier), and the president of the Soviet Union are all members of the Politburo. The Politburo makes all major political, economic, and foreign policy decisions for the Soviet Union. Most members of the Politburo are sixty-five years old or older. All are men.

Most Soviet citizens appear to be content with leaders like this. Czars used to be called "the little father," no matter how cruel. "The little father always knew best," people would say. He had the final say over his "family," the nation. This feeling continues today. The leaders are expected to lead, sometimes with a firm hand, and this is accepted. This idea that some people are meant to be leaders, and others are to be workers and followers, is part of the Russian character. Thus,

World War II was terrible for the Soviet people. These huge statues remind them of the struggles during that time.

there are two "classes" or categories of people. This seems strange in the Soviet Union because its revolution got rid of "classes" and their unequal wealth; in fact, the Soviets still proudly claim that theirs is an equal, "classless society."

Love of Country

Nevertheless, all Soviet citizens are patriotic. They refer to World War II as "the great patriotic war," in which more than twenty million Soviet citizens died, either as soldiers or civilians. It was a war that pulled together the Soviet people to fight a common enemy, regardless of how they felt about their Communist government. They fought bravely for "Mother Russia." Few families escaped the loss of a loved one or a home. This is the chief reason why ordinary Soviet people talk about peace. They know what war is like. At the same time, most people in the Soviet Union do not question their build-up of arms, nor the idea of the draft for all young men who turn eighteen.

Many Soviet citizens are suspicious and sometimes fearful of foreigners. Despite the size and wealth of their country, they feel that the outside world is still "out to get them." They remember how often their country was invaded, beginning with the Vikings and the Bulgars. They remember the invasions by the Tatars, Sweden, Lithuania, and Poland. They remember Napoleon's attack with his 500,000 French soldiers, and, more recently, how Hitler's Nazis devastated their land.

They also remember that the Western Allies of World War I occupied parts of their country in 1917. World War I was still being fought, but the Communists pulled out of the war and made a separate peace with Germany. The Western Allies were angry because Russia had been fighting on their side. The Allies decided to support those Russians who wanted to continue fighting Germany. Soon there was a civil war, with Russian fighting Russian. Fifty thousand French, British, and American soldiers remained on Russian soil for a year. The Americans guarded and transported supplies, but never actually fought any Russians.

This double sense of patriotism and fear of foreigners helps to explain some of the tension between the Soviet Union and its neighbors to the east, south, and west. The Soviets insist that they must protect their borders and air space, because they fear that new invasions might come by way of China, from Iran or Turkey, or out of the West.

And yet, Soviet citizens are often very friendly with foreigners, especially on long train journeys. They love to talk and ask questions. They want to share what they have experienced, and they are curious about the rest of the world.

Talent Everywhere

These qualities—the ability to describe things, and curiosity—have produced an amazing group of writers and other creative artists.

Often their ideas developed in places such as Siberia. Before the Russians began exploring it for minerals, Siberia was a huge, mostly frozen prison camp. Some of the work camps are still there today. The writer Feodor Dostoyevsky spent nine years in Siberia as a convict and a soldier, returning to St. Petersburg to write his novel *Crime and Punishment*. More recently, Alexander Solzhenitsyn, winner of the 1970 Nobel Prize for Literature, experienced a work camp in Siberia (called a *gulag*) which he described in his novel *Gulag Archipelago.*

Alexander Pushkin has been compared to William Shakespeare. Shakespeare's plays and poetry are treasures of the English language; Pushkin was a master of the Russian language. He wrote children's stories, such as "The Golden Cockerel," as well as poetry. Pushkin was black and was quite proud of his racial heritage. His great-grandfather was an African, captured by the Russians as a prisoner-of-war, who later became a general in the Russian army under Peter the Great.

Feodor Dostoyevsky, the writer who served time in Siberia, wrote many novels about interesting people who struggled between being good and being evil. Count Leo Tolstoy wrote historical novels. Tolstoy is most famous for his novel *War and Peace*, which is about Napoleon's invasion of Russia.

You may want to listen to the *1812 Overture* by Peter Tchaikovsky, because it, too, was inspired by Napoleon's invasion. In this work you can hear music from the national anthems of Russia and France "colliding" with one another, along with "cannon fire" symbolizing Napoleon's defeat and retreat. Some orchestra conductors use real cannons for this effect!

Other great musicians include Alexander Borodin, Aram Khachaturian (from Armenia), Serge Prokofief (who wrote a "musical fairy tale," *Peter and the Wolf*), and more modern composers such as Serge Rachmaninoff, Igor Stravinsky, and Dimitri Shostakovich.

Soviet Names

These names aren't easy to pronounce, but they are interesting names. The names of Russian people tell us something of their background and character.

For instance, let's analyze the full name of the famous Russian author *Leo Nikolayevich Tolstoy.*

Leo is his given (or first) name, of course.

That second name is called a *patronymic*, which is common in Russia. This name indicates your father's name. "Nikolayevich" means "son of Nicholas;" thus, it is "Leo, the son of Nicholas."

Tolstoy was a nickname that became the family name. Originally, this family emigrated from Lithuania. Then, the family name was said to have been Indris. As the years passed, in the fifteenth century there was a very fat ancestor who was named "The Stout One." In Russian, that's *Tolstoy*. The name stuck.

Many of the given names are recognizable to us who do not speak Russian. *Ivan* is John. *Yuri*, or *Yurgi*, is George. *Mikhail* is Michael. *Pavel* is Paul. *Sonia* is

Families are very close in the Soviet Union. Children's middle names often come from one of their parents' names.

Sonia—but it comes from the Greek name *Sophronia*. *Alya* is Alice. *Katerina* is Catherine. *Konstantin* is Constantine. *Lisenka* comes from Elizabeth.

Some of the names are more distinctively Russian. *Tatiana*, a girl's name, honors a third-century saint. *Anastasia* honors another saint, and the name, in Greek, means "resurrection." *Feodor* is Francis.

Soviet parents love to use *diminutives* (an example in English is Johnny for John). Thus, many of the names we find in Russian short stories and novels are diminutives. A few examples: *Vanya* (Ivan or John), *Misha* (Michael), *Sasha* (Alexei), *Katya* (Catherine), *Tosha* (Anthony), and *Tanya* (Tatiana).

The Heart of the People

The Soviet people can be very generous, sharing food or giving gifts. They like to treat themselves occasionally, spending an entire week's salary on a meal they share with friends and family.

They are also very sentimental. You see tears and a lot of hugging and kissing in railroad stations as family members say good-bye to each other. It's an old Russian custom for men to kiss men, whether in greeting or farewell. You don't joke about it.

Most Soviet citizens are religious people, despite the official policy of atheism (the teaching that there is no God) in the Communist state. The Soviet Constitution guarantees freedom of worship but insists upon separation of church and state (as does the U.S. Constitution). Many older churches have been turned into museums. Sunday and Sabbath schools are not allowed. Christians, Jews, and Muslims are permitted to worship in churches, synagogues, or mosques which

Religion is important to many Soviet citizens. These women are praying outside a church in Vladimir.

are properly registered with the government. Children are now allowed to attend with their parents. However, they must be eighteen years old before they can join any religious group.

There may be as many as ninety million Soviet citizens who openly practice their faith. Less than twenty million Soviet citizens are official members of the Communist Party, and even some of these will seek out their religious leader—rabbi, pastor, priest, or iman—for special events, especially when a child is born. Religious tradition is still very strong.

The Russian Orthodox Church is a large part of that tradition. Its onion-domed churches dot the country, and, although many of these may now be state museums, the buildings inspire many paintings. The Orthodox Church uses the ancient Slavonic language. Its art, worship services, and beautiful singing without any musical instruments playing continues to influence the Russian character.

The Soviet people have a great love for children. Families are not large, perhaps because living space is still so limited. Usually, there are only one or two children in a family—but the children are important. Some say they are protected too much and even spoiled. Little children are bundled up with the first chilly wind; they wear so many heavy clothes they can't easily bend over. In playgrounds, parents and grandparents rush about to keep their tiny children from falling or getting dirty. Most of the toddlers end up just standing around watching the older children at play.

Children are well fed. Parents provide them with good clothes and many toys. Since both parents must often work, the children are in day care centers or schools for many hours during the week. Parents enjoy special outings with their children on weekends and holidays. The children are included in family activities. You see more smiles and hear more laughter at playgrounds than at any other place in the Soviet Union.

The Soviet Union is big and has much variety in its people as well. Slightly more than half of the people are Russians. The rest are Ukrainians, Moldavians, Uzbeks, Latvians, Lithuanians, Estonians, Armenians, Kazahks, Georgians, and several dozen more. How did all these people come to be citizens of the Soviet Union? To understand any nation we must become acquainted with its people's roots.

3. Tales of Czars and Revolution

Before it had a name, the land we now call Russia was like a magnet, attracting wandering tribes. Some tribes were looking for food. A few were greedy. Others were just on an adventure. What attracted them was the steppe, a flat prairie without trees or other barriers, that had the deepest, richest soil known to humans. Such land meant being able to grow food.

We don't know who the first settlers were. People did live there going back at least thirty centuries, before history was written down. We don't know what language these first settlers spoke; if they could write, no one has yet found any sign of it. We only know that there was much shedding and mixing of blood before a nation was born.

There are a few clues about what happened. The first person to actually write history was a Greek named Herodotus who lived about four hundred years before the birth of Christ. His travels took him to the shores of the Black Sea, the gateway to the steppe.

The first invaders, he told us, were the Scythians, who came from the south, perhaps from Persia. They were expert horseriders and cruel fighters. They drank the blood of the first person they killed or scalped their victims. The Scythians in turn were beaten by the Sarmatians, who were followed by other conquering tribes: the Goths from Germany, the Bulgars from the Balkans, the Huns from Asia, and the Avars from Turkey.

The Slavs and the Vikings

Another tribe lived in the north, in the forests. These were the *Slavs*, who built settlements and cities for protection. They, too, were often under attack from the Khazars in the east and the Finns in the west. The Slavs won and lost battles, absorbed their conquerors, and survived.

The Slavs spoke a language that is the root of modern Russian, as well as Polish, Czech, Byelorussian, Serbian, Wendish, Bulgarian, and Ukrainian. These are called *Slavic* languages.

The ninth century, A.D. was the dawn of written history about Russia. History begins with a man called Rurik who wasn't even a Russian. Rurik was a Viking who captured the Slavic fort of Novgorod in A.D. 862. The Viking people, the first world explorers, were Scandinavian warriors and sailors. They were probably the first Europeans to discover America, perhaps at the same time that others of their tribe were invading Russia.

Novgorod was established before the Soviet Union had a name. Today it has been rebuilt, and is sometimes used as a movie set for historical motion pictures.

Novgorod (which means "the new city") was a trading center built by the Slavs in northwestern "Russia," just south of what is now Leningrad. The Vikings called this area *Rus*, and that may be how the name Russia came to be. Germans and Scandinavians came to Novgorod to trade their goods for furs and *amber*, a jewel-like stone that comes from fossilized tree sap.

When Rurik took Novgorod, the Slavs accepted the Vikings as rulers. For the next 750 years, all of the kings of Russia claimed to be descendants of Rurik. In

A.D. 890 a king named Oleg moved the capital from
Novgorod to Kiev, far to the south on the Dnieper
River. As often happens, the Vikings and the Slavs
intermarried and started to become one people. Oleg's
grandson begins to show this; his name was Svyato*slav*.

The World Beyond Russia

Before there were highways or railroads, the best
way for people to travel was by river. Except for occa-
sional waterfalls or rapids, rivers are mostly smooth,
liquid highways. They have played an important role
in the history of every nation.

The Dnieper River was just such a river-highway in
Russia. To the south of Kiev, it flows into the Black
Sea. From the Black Sea you can sail up the Danube
River past Vienna, Austria and into central Europe.
Also, Istanbul, Turkey is on the Black Sea. Istanbul
was once called Constantinople, and was one of the
most important cities in history.

Traveling north from Kiev on the Dnieper brings
you to the city of Smolensk, and further on to another
river called the Volkhov. The Volkhov takes you to
Novgorod, and beyond it through Lake Ladoga to the
Bay of Finland. Thus, not only was the Dnieper River a
highway inside Russia; it was a connection between
Russia and Europe.

The Russian king sometimes joined his nobles on a yearly trip to Constantinople, the city that linked Europe and Asia. Constantine, the first Roman emperor to become a Christian, had made it the capital of the Roman Empire. Constantinople was named for Constantine. The Russians built boats and filled them with furs, grain, amber, lumber, and other merchandise. They were allowed to enter Constantinople only through a certain gate and could not bring in weapons. They were to sell their goods and slaves as quickly as possible and then return to their homeland.

The Russians were impressed with Constantinople's wealth and culture, as well as with its religion. One hundred years after Rurik's descendants had come to Kiev, King Vladimir of Russia formally accepted Christianity through the Eastern Orthodox Church in Constantinople. He was baptized in the Dnieper River, and forced his subjects to be baptized with him. Kiev for many years was the headquarters for the new Russian Orthodox Church, the official state church of Russia.

In 1220 the Mongols, coming from Asia, attacked the Slavic tribes in the Caucasus, the southwest mountain region of Russia. These Mongols were also called *Tatars*, sometimes spelled "Tartars." The Tatars were led by Genghis Khan, king of Mongolia, whose capital was in China. The Tatars were also called the "Golden Horde." They got that name from their brightly colored

The Dmitrievsky Cathedral was built in the 1100s, soon after King Vladimir converted to Christianity.

tents, which powerfully reflected the gold of the sun. In 1242 the Tatars captured Kiev.

At the same time, the northern Slavic tribes were fighting invading Swedes and Germans. However, the Tatars were in command of all Russia. They taxed the people and set up kingdoms that they controlled. For two centuries they were unchallenged.

Meanwhile, the Slavic kingdom of Muscovy was growing stronger, even though it paid its taxes to the Mongol-Tatars. Moscow, the capital of this kingdom, was growing, and even had a fortress called the Kremlin. The Slavs were preparing for a fight. In 1480, the Tatars were defeated by the king of Muscovy, Ivan III, better known as "Ivan the Great." Moscow now became the capital of all Russia.

The First Czars

The next king was Ivan IV. He was the first Russian king to be crowned *czar*. Czar (sometimes spelled "tsar") was the Russian way of saying "ceasar." Ivan's coronation took place in the Uspensky Cathedral, inside the Kremlin in Moscow.

It's been said that Ivan thought of marrying Queen Elizabeth of England, but instead married a Russian girl from the Romanov family. A hundred years and six kings later, the *Romanov dynasty* was firmly established. A dynasty is a line of rulers from the same family. Russia has had only two dynasties or royal families: the Ruriks and the Romanovs.

Ivan IV had another name, "Ivan the Terrible." The Russian word for terrible is *grozny*, which really means "someone to be dreaded." As we shall see, there were Russian rulers who would be more terrible and cruel than Ivan, even in the twentieth century, but the name has persisted.

Ivan was a warrior who freed the Volga region from raiders. He fought the Swedes in the north and the Livonians in the west, as well as conquering lands in what is now Siberia. Ivan believed in the "divine right of kings." This means that kings can do no wrong, and that rulers have complete power over their subjects. Perhaps this explains why, in many ages, some kings were so cruel.

Because Ivan had complete power, he was able to make any law he liked. One law he made was that peasants had to stay on the land they farmed and could not leave. These peasants were called *serfs*. Serfs and their families would remain chained to the land for almost three hundred years. The taxes paid and the work done by serfs would help land-owning Russians stay wealthy for centuries.

The West Comes to Russia

Two hundred years would pass before another king like Ivan would appear. His name was Peter, and he would be known as "Peter the Great."

Peter was a huge man, nearly seven feet tall. He was curious about everything. To find out how shoes were made, he became a shoemaker. His working as a carpenter and as a bricklayer allowed him to build both cottages and palaces. He mended his own clothes. He learned to be a blacksmith, a printer, and even a drummer!

Peter picked up most of these skills from foreigners who lived in Moscow. Unlike others, he wasn't suspicious or afraid of foreigners. In fact, he wanted to learn more about the West. Peter was the first Russian king to visit the West. He was supposed to be in disguise, but it was easy for people to guess who this giant really was. He lived in Holland for a time. In England, he worked in a shipyard for a while, in addition to visiting the British parliament. Peter returned to Russia to defeat the Turks and to build a navy. He brought many modern ways to Russia. But there was a dark side to his reign.

Peter had always been cruel. As a child, he used real people in playing "soldiers;" many were wounded and some were even killed. As Peter grew older, things became worse. He adopted the more impressive title of "Emperor of the Russian Empire." St. Petersburg, his new capital, was built at the cost of many human lives. He made life worse for the serfs; their masters could now imprison or exile them. Peter's own son, Alexis, was tortured and died in prison. Still, Peter's fascination with the West would have a lasting effect on Russia.

Leningrad, once called St. Petersburg, was built on marshland next to the Neva River. Peter the Great made it the capital of Russia and lived there with his court.

Peter's work was completed by Catherine the Great. She was a German princess (born Sophia of Anhalt-Zerbst) who married Peter's grandson, Peter III. This younger Peter was weak and short on ability. After only six months on the throne, he was removed as czar by the army and was later murdered. His widow became empress.

Catherine, the German princess, loved Russia and its language, and the Russians came to admire her in return. She built roads and bridges. She encouraged education and new industries. Catherine was the first person in Russia to be vaccinated against smallpox, setting an example for her subjects. She arranged for the first Russian settlement in Alaska. Under her, the army absorbed the Ukraine, Crimea, and part of Poland into the Russian empire.

Invasions and Rebellions

The years after Catherine's death were not good for Russian royalty. Her son Paul was murdered, and her grandson Alexander may have had his hand in that crime. Alexander I ruled for twenty-four years and tried to improve conditions. He got rid of the secret police that Ivan the Terrible had begun, as well as the censorship of newspapers. Political prisoners were released. Alexander wanted to free the serfs, but this would not happen during his lifetime. Russian colonies were expanded in Alaska; two were even established in California.

His good intentions were stopped by having to fight Napoleon Bonaparte, the emperor of France who had already conquered Europe. Napoleon marched on Russia with over half a million of his best troops. A major battle was fought at Borodino, a village west of Moscow, in which there were eighty thousand deaths.

Napoleon continued his march all the way to Moscow. By the time he arrived, only a few thousand people remained in the city. Fires broke out, and within four days the entire city was in ruins, except the Kremlin. This was September, 1812.

Winter was coming, and Napoleon offered to make peace. Czar Alexander would not agree to end the war, so Napoleon, despite his victory, was forced to retreat. He had lost too many troops, and now he had no food or supplies for those who remained. His retreat became a defeat. Later, Russia would join other European countries in defeating Napoleon entirely.

Meanwhile, there was much unrest in Russia. A group of young army officers wanted a constitution. They wanted to end serfdom and begin land reform, which would mean giving land to the peasants. Some even wanted to end the monarchy and establish a republic.

Alexander I died on December 13, 1825. Since Alexander had no children, his brother Nicholas was made czar. Due to some confusion, Nicholas did not assume power for several days. The revolutionaries decided the time had come to rebel. They did so on December 26, the day after Christmas. This "Decembrist Revolt" was poorly planned, and Nicholas put it down the same day. Several army leaders were executed; others were exiled.

Nicholas I was the complete opposite of Alexander. There would be no talk of a constitution nor of freeing the serfs during his thirty-year reign. Censorship and the secret police returned; university life was strictly controlled; a rebellion in Poland was crushed; and Siberia became a giant prison camp which held those who disagreed with the czar.

But the seeds of rebellion had been planted and would grow.

Nicholas's son, Alexander II, is known as the "Czar Liberator." He freed the serfs in 1861, two years before slaves were freed in the United States. He organized local governing councils on which even peasants were represented. These councils had the power to set local taxes. Justices of the peace were authorized. Alaska, now a burden to Russia, was sold to the United States.

For many Russians, these reforms came too late or did not go far enough. They wanted a constitution and a congress. The good king Alexander was killed by a terrorist's bomb.

Alexander's two successors would never be as liberal as he was. Alexander III vowed to crush the revolutionaries who had killed his father. He also allowed violent attacks on Jews, called *pogroms.* The son of Alexander III, Nicholas II, would be the last czar of Russia.

Czar Nicholas II and his family, all of whom were executed after the 1917 revolution.

The Early Communists

New political parties were being formed, some of them in line with ideas first raised by Karl Marx, a German refugee in England. Marx wrote about a coming class struggle that would pit rich against poor, and believed that workers would create a communist state—that is, a state owned and run by everyone.

One of the early Marxist leaders in Russia was Vladimir Ilyich Ulianov, who chose to change his last name to Lenin. He called for a general strike in 1905 after Russia lost a brief war with Japan. The strike caused Czar Nicholas to proclaim a constitution and allow a congress (called the *Duma*) to meet. Four congresses were elected over the next twelve years; each congress changed the decisions of the other. There was total chaos, encouraged by such leaders as Lenin, who, following the ideas of Karl Marx, believed that total revolution, not laws, was the answer. Then the First World War began.

Russia was joined by the Allies in fighting Germany. Russia lost important battles, and blame again fell on Czar Nicholas, who finally gave up the throne both for himself and his son. His brother Michael could have become the new czar, but refused. A provisional (temporary) government was formed. It included one man who was socialist but no Communists. Lenin fled to Finland when his group failed to take over the government.

This was the end of the Romanov dynasty and the Russian monarchy. Nicholas II and his family would later be murdered.

The provisional government was a republic, first led by Prince George Lvov, then by a socialist, Alex-

Before the revolution, soldiers and workers formed soviets (councils) for lawmaking. Most soldiers participated in overthrowing the czar.

ander Kerensky. This temporary government lasted less than eight months. Lenin, with the backing of soldiers and workers in Petrograd, returned from Finland to direct a takeover. He said, "History will not forgive us if we do not seize power now." In 1917 the Bolshevik members of Lenin's party, the Social Democrats (a socialist party), took control. Bolshevik in Russian means "majority." The Bolsheviks were Communists. Lenin became head of the government.

All land became the property of the state; banks were taken over by the government, too. The national debt was not honored. Factories became the property of the state, and workers were instructed to join the government trade unions. Church property was seized.

Lenin signed a peace treaty with Germany. Under this agreement, Russia had to give up three states on the Baltic Sea and part of Poland to Germany. Also, the Ukraine was granted independence, for a time. The next year, civil war broke out between the "Reds" and the "Whites"—between the Communists and those who opposed them. The Whites were helped by the Allies of World War I, who even occupied a few parts of Russia. But the people supported the Reds, and the Whites soon lost.

V.I. Lenin, who led the Russian Revolution, was the first leader of the country. Here he speaks in Red Square in 1919.

In 1922 Russia became the Union of Soviet Socialist Republics, when the states of the Ukraine, Byelorussia (White Russia), and Transcaucasia formed a federation.

The Stalin Era

Since 1917 there have been only a few leaders of the Soviet Union.

Lenin, the "father of his country," died in 1924. A struggle for power developed between Leon Trotsky and Joseph Stalin. Stalin won out. Trotsky was exiled to Siberia, then exiled from the Soviet Union, and eventually assassinated in Mexico.

Stalin remained in power from Lenin's death until 1953. His real name was Joseph Djugashvili; the adopted name of Stalin means "like steel." Stalin was indeed as tough as steel as a leader. He was once compared to Peter the Great. Both were hard, cruel dictators; both helped modernize their country.

Collective and state farms, where all products were common property, were begun in 1928. These huge areas of land were now owned by the government and often worked by the former owners. *Kulaks* (farmers) who still owned land and refused to cooperate were killed or exiled. Under Stalin there was a large-scale *purge* of the Communist Party, too. One million people were thrown out of the Party. Some disappeared. Many were executed, including old-time veteran Communist leaders.

Stalin could also be underhanded. He signed treaties with Estonia, Latvia, and Lithuania, but later occupied the three Baltic states. Stalin signed another treaty with Adolf Hitler, the German dictator, but Hitler broke that treaty. His Nazi army invaded the Soviet Union in 1941.

World War II was a terrible time for the Soviet people. Hitler's army reached the Volga River in the east, and Leningrad in the north. Moscow itself was in danger. Twenty million Soviet soldiers and civilians were killed in what the Soviets call their "great patriotic war." When the Nazis retreated, what remained of cities and villages was burned and destroyed so that the Nazis would have no food or shelter. Little was left but scorched earth. There was fierce fighting in the Soviet Union for four long years. Their Allies sent them food, trucks, and weapons to help them in their fight. As the Western Allies—Great Britain, France, the United States, and others—pushed east from France, the Soviet armies marched west, capturing Berlin. American and Soviet soldiers finally met at Torgau, Germany, on the banks of the Elbe River. In Europe, the war was over. Some months later Japan surrendered, and World War II was ended.

European Geography Changes

A few months before the German defeat, Joseph Stalin met with U.S. President Franklin Roosevelt and British Prime Minister Winston Churchill at Yalta, a resort on the Black Sea. The three Allied leaders drew up agreements on terms for Germany's surrender and on areas of influence for each Allied country. The various countries that had been under Germany's rule were to be helped and governed for a time by each of the Allies. That meeting helped determine the present geography and politics of Europe. A *bloc* (group) of countries would be the Soviet Union's responsibility. This bloc included the eastern half of Germany, Albania, Poland, Czechoslovakia, Hungary, Bulgaria, Romania, and Yugoslavia. Also at this meeting, Stalin agreed to enter the war against Japan.

After the fighting was finally ended—the "hot war"—a new war began, the "Cold War." This was a war for influence and power. The people involved mostly used words and threats or sent troops to fight in small wars. The Soviet Union believed that its form of government was best; the other Allies disagreed. The Soviets used their influence from World War II to set up Communist governments in all the countries that had been put in their care. In some places the Soviets even sent in soldiers and tanks to stop people who fought against these "satellite" governments. The Soviet Union also used its power in these countries to cut off most contact between its bloc and the free Western countries. Churchill named this the "Iron Curtain."

The Communist and the Western blocs each tried to get ahead of the other, sometimes coming very close to fighting. At one time the Soviet Union cut off free West Berlin from the rest of West Germany. The United States and its allies had to fly in food and other goods until the Soviets stopped their blockade. A few years after the war, the Western nations formed the North Atlantic Treaty Organization, a joint military group; in response, the Soviet Union and its bloc established the Warsaw Pact, a similar group. In 1949 the Soviet Union exploded its first atomic bomb. Up until that time, only the United States had possessed that weapon. Soon after, the Soviet Union and the United States started an arms race, each trying to build more and better weapons than the other. Each country wanted to be safe by being stronger than its opponents.

Khrushchev Comes to Power

Joseph Stalin died in 1953. For two years no one person held all the power in the country. Georgi Malnekov was Soviet premier; after him came Nikolai Bulganin. But the leader who eventually ended up on top

Nikita Khrushchev addressing the United Nations General Assembly in 1960. Four years later he lost his power and was forced out as premier.

was Nikita Khrushchev, who headed the Soviet Union from about 1956 to 1964.

During Khrushchev's time in office, things were sometimes better and sometimes worse. People did not have to live in terror as they did when Joseph Stalin was in power. Khrushchev said publicly that Stalin had been wrong in many ways, and tried to get rid of people Stalin appointed as well as memories of the man himself. Khrushchev even allowed some limited contact with the West; cultural exchanges of Soviet musicians and dancers were made with Western countries.

The first person to orbit the earth in space, cosmonaut Yuri Gagarin. Cosmonaut means "sailor of the universe;" astronaut means "sailor among the stars."

However, the Cold War continued. The Soviets put the first satellite and the first person into space. Then began a "space race" between the Soviet Union and the United States in addition to the arms race. The United States sent a spy plane over the Soviet Union; the Soviets shot it down and captured its pilot, becoming very angry about the whole incident. A couple of years later, the Soviet Union placed missiles on Cuba, just ninety miles from U.S. shores. The United States stopped all ships going to Cuba until the Russians agreed to remove the missiles.

Years of Détente

Khrushchev somewhat improved relations between East and West. However, he lost power because
his plans for improving manufacturing and agriculture
had failed, and because some Communist nations,
most importantly China, had withdrawn from the Communist bloc. In 1964 Leonid Brezhnev became Party
head, and Alexei Kosygin became premier. These two
spent their first years in power changing the way goods
and foods were produced. Brezhnev eventually became
the more powerful of the two.

All this time, the United States and the Soviet
Union had been building more and more nuclear weapons. In the late 1960s both agreed to talk about
reducing the weapons they had. The Strategic Arms
Limitation Talks (SALT) began in 1969. An agreement
for reducing arms was signed in 1972.

The SALT agreement was one sign that relations
between the two countries were better. This easing of
tensions was called *détente*. Besides the arms control
agreement, the two countries also agreed to share some
medical and scientific knowledge, as well as allowing
more cultural exchanges of performers. Probably the
most well-known example of U.S.-Soviet cooperation
was a joint space flight. An American Apollo space
capsule met up with a Soviet Soyuz capsule out in

space. For two days the capsules remain joined together as American astronauts and Soviet cosmonauts performed scientific experiments as a team. Later the capsules unhooked and came down separately.

The 1970s were marked by dissent within the Soviet Union and continued Soviet involvement in other countries' affairs. There were protests against the difficulty of emigrating by Soviet Jews and others in religious groups. Eventually the government decided to grant exit visas to some of those who wanted to leave the country for good. Other protests surfaced from some of the non-Russian-speaking minorities in the republics, who wanted more power for themselves and an end to discrimination. Sill other dissent came from some Soviet *intelligentsia*, who were asking the government to allow more personal freedom and to stop its cruel treatment of people who disagreed with government policies. Sometimes dissenters were sent to Siberian work camps. Sometimes dissenters were put into mental hospitals to be "cured." Some, like writer Alexander Solzhenitsyn, lost their Soviet citizenship. Others, like scientist Andrei Sakharov, were placed under "house" arrest, and not allowed to move around or to have any contact with the outside world.

During both the 1960s and the 1970s the Soviet Union stepped up its aid to other countries, often located in less well-developed areas of the world. Some-

In spite of modern machinery and many workers, the Soviet Union was forced to buy grain several times in the 1970s after Soviet crops failed.

times Soviet scientists would help the people of the country learn better farming techniques and methods of manufacturing goods. Sometimes Soviet advisors helped on projects like building dams or roads. In later years, though, the Soviet Union would send military advisors, troops, or weapons to countries whose government was friendly to them. In doing this, the Soviets would help that government stay in power, no matter if the people of the country wanted that government or not. The Soviet Union became involved in such places as the Middle East, Africa, and Central America. They often aided countries which opposed the United States or its allies.

In 1979 the Soviet government ordered an invasion of Afghanistan to support the pro-Soviet government in power and to keep a civil war from happening on its border. Many countries protested this, especially the United States. The United States withdrew its support for a second SALT agreement. They stopped exporting food to the Soviet Union. The United States also led a boycott of the 1980 Summer Olympics which were being held in Moscow.

In 1980 Kosygin died; in 1982 Brezhnev died. Yuri Andropov became Party head and then president, but died in 1984. Konstantin Chernenko then came into power. In the 1980s the Soviet Union led protests of the United States' involvement in a civil war in El

Salvador. They also boycotted the 1984 Summer Olympic Games held in Los Angeles. In 1983 Soviet fighter jets fired upon and shot down a Korean airliner that strayed over its air space. It has also continued its experiments in space, sending cosmonauts to live in spaceships for long periods of time in hopes of someday having factories there. The Soviet Union again lost its leader in 1985 when Chernenko died. Mikhail Gorbachev then replaced him.

Russia came out of isolation with Peter the Great. It showed its strength in defeating Napoleon. In World War II the country showed its spirit again, fighting alone to Germany's east so that the Allies could fight their way west. Today, the Soviet Union is a major world power, a nation that commands both respect and fear.

4. The Storytellers

Surviving in Russia, for the common people, has always required a sense of humor and much patience.

The country had no constitution until the beginning of the 1900s. Laws were made by one person's orders, and were the result of the whim of a king or a local noble. Freedom was hard to find and keep. Because the people had to be so careful, criticism of the government often took the form of stories. Sometimes the stories were satire; sometimes they were humorous. That same sort of humor continues today. Here are some recent political jokes from the Soviet Union.

A man goes to a doctor's office.

"I must see an ear and eye doctor!" he shouts.

"But you've come to the wrong place," says the receptionist. "This is an ear, nose, and throat clinic."

"But I must see an ear and eye doctor!"

"Why?"

"Because what I hear is not what I see."

Pravda, the Communist Party newspaper published in Moscow, is running a contest for the best political joke. The first prize is twenty years in Siberia.

For many years, wandering entertainers told stories and sang for people in the countrysides. The two men here are acting out an old folk tale.

Jokes and Heroes

In olden days, such stories and jokes were told by wandering entertainers. They sang songs or ballads called *byliny*, or they told folktales called *shazki*. In these performances, the czars were never openly criticized; the entertainer would pretend that the czar was either very young and inexperienced, or very old and a bit stupid. The smartest people in their stories were peasants and children.

Heroes in old Russia were often knights, but not always; these heroes were called *bogatyrs*. If you remember that the Russian word for God is *bog*, then you get the idea that a knight was a kind of superhuman person, who had great strength. One of these hero-knights praised by the wandering entertainers sounds a lot like our Paul Bunyan. His name was Saint Gregory the Brave. Whenever he moved, a great noise was heard from the North. The forests quaked. Mother Earth trembled. Streams gushed out from steep banks. Gregory was taller than the forests through which he walked. He could lift the earth on his shoulders. He carried his wife in a tiny crystal chest.

Other ballads were sung about peasant-heroes such as Mikula, Oleg (who was named for the Volga River), and Dunai Ivanovich (named for the Don River). Another famous hero was Samson Samoylovich, a kind of Russian Hercules.

There were also songs and stories about Slavic gods. Perhaps the Vikings brought with them the worship of Thor, the Thunder-God. The Russians called him *Perun*; the Lithuanians called him *Perkunas*. The Russian god of cattle was named *Volos*, the god of wealth was *Dazhbog*, the god of winds was named

Stribog, and the god of a clear sky was *Svarog*. (Note the Russian word *bog,* or god, in some of these names.)

Other ballads and stories were created about the Cossacks. In the past few years, Cossack entertainer groups have visited the United States and Canada. In their shows they wear colorful embroidered shirts, homespun pants, fur hats, and shiny black boots while they sing and dance. The Cossack dance is an energetic, leg-kicking movement from a squatting position. However, the Cossacks of long ago were much more than exciting dancers and singers. They were brave and fierce warriors.

Originally, they were nomads from Turkey who rode horses. They lived on the edges of civilization in Russia. Escaped serfs sometimes joined them, and adopted Cossack dress, while the Cossacks adopted their Russian language. Cossacks have always been free; none was ever a slave. The region where they lived was a refuge for Russians who were being cruelly treated. Eventually, the Cossacks migrated to the steppes, the flatlands of the eastern Ukraine. They started a frontier colony, where they avoided farming when they could in favor of hunting. They were always ready to hire themselves out as soldiers. Cossacks were the backbone of Catherine the Great's army. It's not surprising that these colorful and exciting people have been responsible for so many legends.

Fairytales

It's said that more fairytales are told in Russia than anywhere else in the world. One such story is called "The Silver Saucer and the Transparent Apple." You may think it sounds like a "Cinderella" story.

There were three sisters. The youngest was the most beautiful and the hardest worker. We'll call her Anna. The older sisters were mean and lazy, and they called their younger sister "Little Stupid."

One day, their father was going to the market in Novgorod. He asked his daughters what they would like him to bring back as presents. One older sister wanted a necklace. Another wanted a gold-hemmed dress. Anna asked for a silver saucer and a transparent apple. Her father raised his eyebrows, sighed, and went on his way. He returned with all of the gifts, although he admitted that finding a silver saucer and a transparent apple wasn't the easiest thing in the world.

Anna began to spin the transparent apple on the silver saucer, and it became a kind of crystal ball. As it spun, Anna looked at it and saw Moscow, and ships, and even the czar. Her father leaned over and he saw the Novgorod market, where he had just been. It was magic, and the older sisters were furious that they didn't own such a wonderful thing.

The sisters plotted to steal Anna's gift. They invited Anna to go berry-hunting with them, and to bring her silver saucer and transparent apple with her. Anna suspected some mischief and asked her father to take care of her prized possession.

There was no berry-hunting. None had been planned. Instead, the two older sisters murdered Anna, buried her, and then sobbed to their father that Anna must have run off and gotten lost in the forest. The father searched for her but could not find her.

Months passed by; then a reed grew on top of Anna's grave. A shepherd boy passing by cut the reed and began to whittle a flute. As he was whittling, the reed began to sing on its own. It was the voice of Anna, and she told of her murder. She asked that someone tell her parents. When her father heard this story, he rushed to the grave, where the reed continued its sing-song story. Anna said she could be helped only if water from the czar's own well were poured over her grave.

The older sisters heard all of this, were very frightened, and confessed their crime. The townspeople were ready to hang them, but their father pleaded that they be spared. He had lost Anna and he still wanted to have some children. The villagers listened to the father, and did not harm his older daughters.

After a few days, the father journeyed to the czar's palace, saw the king, and told him the whole story. The czar gave the father a glass of water from his well and said he would like to see Anna if she ever awakened.

The father carefully carried that glass of water back to his village. The grave was opened and the water was sprinkled. Magically, Anna awakened.

The whole family journeyed to the czar's palace to thank the king for his kindness. The czar was pleased to see Anna. He asked to see the magical saucer and apple. As the apple spun, the king could see his entire kingdom. He was amazed. He could count his soldiers, see all of his cities, and even look for approaching enemies. By this time the czar was very taken with the beauty of Anna and asked her to marry him. She agreed, but insisted that her sisters and parents be allowed to live in the palace with her. We can assume that they all lived happily ever after.

The Wicked Witch

All fairy stories must have a wicked witch, and the Russian version deserves a special prize. She's called *Baba Yaga.* Many stories are told about her.

Baba Yaga is very ugly. She looks like a bag of bones. Her eyes flash. She has iron teeth. She eats up bad children, but the good ones get away.

Baba Yaga lives in a hut that has legs like a hen's. Those legs actually move, so sometimes the hut faces

Baba Yaga is the Russian wicked witch. She lives in a hut that has chicken legs, and travels in a mortar with a pestle!

the forest, and sometimes the path. The hut can also move to some totally new location.

Baba Yaga has an amazing vehicle for travel. In an older drug store, a chemistry laboratory, or a health food store you may have seen a mortar and a pestle. A mortar is a kind of bowl. A pestle is a tool—a bar or stick. A mortar and pestle is used to grind down crystals and other hard substances into powder. Well, Baba Yaga travels inside a flying mortar, getting more speed by beating it with a pestle. She also carries a small twig broom, called a besom, with which she sweeps over her tracks to erase them.

Many libraries have collections of other Russian stories. You might like to read about Sadko, Prince Ivan, the Witch Baby, the Snow Maiden, or the Flying Ship. Two stories by Alexander Pushkin are full of magic and fun: *The Tales of Czar Sultan* and *The Golden Cockerel.*

Russian Proverbs

Nikita Khrushchev once headed the Soviet Union. He loved to drop Russian proverbs into his conversations and even into his speeches. (A proverb is a well-known saying.) The patience and the wit of the Russian people is captured in such sayings.

Some examples:

V. I. Lenin, pictured on this huge outdoor mural in Leningrad, is an honored hero to the Soviet people.

"In a fight, the rich man tries to save his face, the poor man his coat."

"Long whiskers cannot take the place of brains."

"He who digs a hole for another may fall in himself." (Khrushchev often quoted this one.)

"Peeling an egg does not put it in your mouth."

There is much wisdom in these sayings. And some of them reflect a way of thinking that is typically Russian.

"The tears of strangers are only water."

"When you live next to the cemetery, you cannot weep for everyone."

"Pray to God but continue to row to the shore."

And a favorite: "Better to turn back than to lose your way."

5. Patriotic Holidays and Family Fun

Most official holidays in the Soviet Union are linked with national patriotic events. The others have to do with the seasons or with culture. Religious holidays are celebrated, but they are in no way official.

The most important holiday in the Soviet Union is its "Independence Day," celebrated on November 7. Actually, it's called the *Great October Revolution Day*. Why is October remembered in November? The answer's in the calendar.

Different countries didn't always follow the same calendar. This made things complicated and explains both why we don't have the same number of days each month and why we have an extra day every four years during a leap year. Most of the world, including the Soviet Union, now does its business by the Gregorian Calendar. This calendar began in 1582. However, during the reign of the Russian czars, the Julian Calendar, an older calendar, was followed, which was thirteen days "behind" the rest of us. According to that Julian Calendar, the provisional government in Petrograd was overthrown on October 24 and 25, 1917. Czar Nicholas had already given up the throne. This Octobrist Revolution was the beginning of the modern

Soviet Union. Using the new calendar, it's now remembered officially in November.

The holiday is celebrated throughout the nation, but the major events take place in Moscow and Leningrad. The festivities there are televised to all parts of the Soviet Union.

Moscow is decorated with bunting, streamers, and flags. It is a day of parades, most of it dedicated to the armed forces. A huge military band plays thoughout the day. The Soviet leaders stand on top of the Lenin Mausoleum (tomb) reviewing the troops and their military equipment.

After the soldiers, marines, sailors, tanks, and rockets have passed, it's time for the gymnasts to perform. They are followed by dance groups from each of the fifteen republics. Children also parade proudly. Some of them are just tiny toddlers. They walk in single file, carrying red flags.

Finally, workers from farms and factories march in front of the reviewing stand. Many of the workers carry their children on their shoulders. The parade lasts all day and sometimes into the night. As the skies darken, the buildings are lit up. When the parade is finally over, fireworks streak across the sky.

On Revolution Day in Leningrad, a large part of the Soviet fleet anchors in the Neva River, just across from the former Winter Palace. The ships are brightly

Children often participate in parades, showing their dancing or athletic abilities.

lit. Thousands of people come to see them, even though it can be quite cold in early November.

Other Patriotic Days

The next most important political holiday is *May Day*, held on May 1. In 1889, socialists in France began the tradition of making May 1 their "Labor Day." It is not primarily a day to display military power—instead, it is a day of family fun. There are parades, of course. The armed forces march, and workers carry banners and huge papier-maché statues and puppets. The groups that march form in neighborhoods and then join together in the central city.

Schoolchildren play an important part in May Day celebrations. It is a great honor for them to march and to show their gymnastic abilities. The parades are followed by pageants and sports displays in various parts of the city.

Another patriotic holiday celebrated in May is *VE Day*. *VE* stands for "Victory in Europe," or the end of World War II in Europe. This has tremendous meaning for the Soviet people, who suffered so much in their "great patriotic war." Again, there is a strange difference in dates. The Soviet people celebrate VE Day on May 9, although Hitler's armies surrendered on May 8, 1945. Joseph Stalin, the Soviet leader at the time, did not announce the armistice for twenty-four hours, although Soviet generals had already signed the peace agreement with the Germans in Berlin. The reason for the delay is still a mystery, but the celebration of the war's end continues throughout the Soviet Union, regardless of the date.

Seasonal Holidays

In the Soviet Union there are harvest festivals in the fall which celebrate the end of work in the fields.

They are another happy excuse for parades, dancing, sports events, and picnics.

The *Russian Winter Festival* lasts twelve days, from December 25 to January 5. Although Christmas is not officially recognized, there are some similarities with Christmas celebrations. Evergreen trees are sold and are decorated in the homes—but they are called "New Year's Trees." There is somebody who looks like Santa Claus, but he isn't called St. Nicholas—he is *Dyed Maroz* or "Grandfather Frost." He wears a red suit and white beard.

New Year's Day is the most important holiday during the Winter Festival. It may be the most exciting family holiday of the year. There are carnivals, winter sports, and special performances of circuses. This is the day when toys are given to the children.

Religious Holidays

During December, Christmas is celebrated by Christians and Chanukah by Jewish people. However, these religious holidays are limited to private homes or to houses of prayer (which is often the name for a church or synagogue). Christmas cards are not exchanged because none are printed in the Soviet Union.

Easter and Passover are also celebrated quietly, not publicly. Special foods are prepared, especially cakes and cookies, which are enjoyed for several days after Easter.

A special Easter cake that is baked is called *koulich*. It's a lot like a white cake, but it has raisins, chopped nuts, and chopped candied fruits. It's frosted and sometimes the letters "KV" are etched into the icing. *KV* stands for *Khristos voskress*. These Russian words mean "Christ is Risen." On Easter Sunday, Soviet Christians greet each other with those words. One will say, "Khristos voskress!" and the other will reply, "Voistinu voskress!" (which means "He is risen indeed!") The words are frequently shouted between priest and people during the Easter worship services.

Ukrainians are famous for their craft of decorating Easter eggs, called *pysanky*. The eggs are not cooked or blown out, but will eventually dry out if left uncovered. The symbols on the eggs are significant. Waves and ribbons symbolize life without end. The fish, the cross, the triangle, and the star refer to God or to Christ. Children enjoy learning to decorate these eggs. It is an art which requires practice and skill. The decorated eggs are given as Easter gifts and are then displayed with pride throughout the year.

Soviet Muslims celebrate the ninth month of their calendar as *Ramadan*. This is a time of fasting and meditation, from sunrise to sunset, every day for twenty-eight days. When the new moon appears, the fasting ends and a celebration begins which lasts for several days. It's called the "Little Festival" and there is much feasting and exchanging of gifts.

Family Holidays and Gatherings

Around the world, the best holidays are usually family vacations. These are special times for Soviet families. Since both parents often work, vacations are times when all of the family can be together, twenty-four hours a day, for two or more weeks.

An izba, or cabin, is sometimes rented for family vacations.

Time together is precious to Soviet families. Parents and children enjoy sharing activities such as ice skating.

If they like to swim, they will travel to seashores on the Baltic, Black, or Caspian seas. If they like to camp and hike, they may go to the mountains or forests. More campgrounds are being built. Perhaps the family will be able to rent an *izba* (cabin) in the countryside. Maybe the family will decide to take a riverboat trip. They might also visit a large city and sightsee, taking in the museums, circuses, the ballet, or a puppet show.

Perhaps the family will plan its visit to a major city to see one of the popular city festivals. The *Festival of Moscow Stars* is held in May. The *Leningrad White Nights* are held in June. ("White nights" refer to the longest days of the year, when there is still sunlight at

10 p.m.!) The *Riga Song Festival* is in August. And, of course, there are national and international games in soccer and hockey, as well as skating meets.

One of the things children can enjoy on their trips are "Children's Railroads." There are thirty of them in the Soviet Union, but the best-known one is in Kiev. The only adult on these railroads is the train engineer. Everything else is run by children—the three stations, the ticket office, and the signal boxes. In the wintertime, these children may join a railroad club in their city, where they build model railroads and learn more about railroading.

Whatever they decide to do with their free time, it is very unlikely that the family will take its vacation outside of the Soviet Union. Foreign travel is mostly restricted to official and scientific meetings. Sometimes cultural exchange groups and friendship groups are allowed to go out of the country. Of course, the family doesn't have to travel anywhere. Sometimes it's fun just to stay at home and explore one's own city and countryside. Soviet citizens enjoy visiting parks and playgrounds, or going on long hikes, even if these are close to home.

One of the popular activities to do on a hike is *mushrooming.* You must be very certain of what mushrooms to collect, because some are poisonous. Soviet parents have learned from long experience which mushrooms are edible, and they pass this knowledge to their children. The mushrooms are usually dried and stored for use in the winter.

The happiest family event of all is a wedding of a relative or friend. A wedding requires lots of planning and preparation, and everyone gets involved. The wedding itself is conducted by an official in a government wedding palace. The building can be quite beautiful,

Marriages often take place in special wedding palaces.

but often the ceremonies are very brief because there are long lines of couples waiting to be married. A few couples also choose to arrange for some religious blessing of their marriage, in either a church or synagogue. Hundreds of people may be invited.

Every wedding guest is expected to bring a flower. Just a single flower. There are flower stands nearby where you can purchase your flower at almost any time of the year. After the wedding ceremony, a reception line is formed so that the bride and groom may be greeted. The flowergirl (or boy) stands beside the couple, with both arms held out. As the guests pass by, they place their flower on those outstretched arms. The children get very tired from holding several dozen flowers!

After the wedding is the party, with food and fun, dancing, meeting old friends and getting to know new ones, and lots of laughter and music. Weddings always remind us that life goes on, that love and hope are good reasons to celebrate.

6. Of Dachas, Rubles and Borscht

What is it like to be a member of a family in the Soviet Union?

First of all, a child will probably have only one brother or sister. Most Soviet families are small and housing is still very crowded, although improving. You already know about the destruction caused by the Second World War. Over forty years later, the Soviet Union still suffers from a housing shortage, but it is beginning to catch up.

Housing and Property

A few years ago, an official Soviet plan called for providing one apartment for each family. That apartment might consist of only one or two rooms, and its tenants would have to share cooking and washing facilities with other families in the building. In such a small place, sofa beds and folding cots are used for sleeping, then pushed aside for a dining area in the daytime. Today, the plan is to build enough new buildings so that there will be a room for each citizen.

People who work in factories usually live in apartment complexes that are built nearby. Often these

These workers probably live near their factory, because apartment buildings are often built near workplaces.

industrial "parks"—factories plus housing—are built in the countryside, far from any city. You see many new apartment buildings in the cities, or their suburbs. They are mostly high-rise buildings. Some of these new apartment complexes are condominiums—which is something new for the Soviet Union. You make a down payment, pay a monthly fee, and, in time, you will own your own apartment. You cannot sell your apartment to anyone else, but you can sell it back to the government agency that built it.

It is sometimes possible to own personal property in the Soviet Union. Some individuals have inherited family homes. People live in houses, rather than apartments, in the rural villages.

A few privileged people own *dachas*, or country homes, as well as an apartment in the city. Such persons are usually government officials, cosmonauts, scientists, and other "very important people." It's estimated that 30 percent of housing in the Soviet Union is privately owned. The rest is rented from the government. However, no one owns land, not even the land on which a homestead or village house is located.

All land belongs to the government. Farmers who work on the gigantic, government-owned collective farms are allowed to plant gardens on an acre or two, to raise chickens, or even to keep a cow. They are permitted to sell any extra products from those they raise for themselves. But they do not own this land, either. It's given to them on a kind of lease.

More families than ever before now own an automobile. However, there are only twenty-four cars for every thousand people in the Soviet Union (compared with 526 cars for every thousand people in the United States) so there still isn't much of a traffic problem. In fact, a person must sign up on a waiting list and may be able to buy a new car after two or three years.

The automobiles sold are manufactured in the Soviet Union. The name of the most expensive limousine is the *Zil*. A smaller luxury car, used by officials, is the *Chaika*. Intermediate-size cars are called *Volgas*; many of these are government-owned taxis. A compact *Fiat-*

125 is what ordinary people buy, if they can afford
7,500 rubles.

Soviet industry manufactures its own refrigerators, washing machines, cooking stoves, radios, television sets, and small appliances. There may also be a
waiting list to purchase these items. There is only one
"brand," with no competition and no advertising.

Money and Salaries

Soviet citizens purchase things with *rubles* and
kopeks. There are a hundred kopeks in a ruble. The
ruble and kopek were used in the days of the czars. The
word *ruble* originally meant "a block of wood," so
perhaps the early coins were something like wooden
nickels. "Kopek" means "lance." The early kopek coins
showed the czar riding a horse and carrying a lance. A
ruble is worth more than a U.S. dollar (about $1.20).

Monthly salaries range from about 100 to 500
rubles. That maximum is paid even to high government officials, but they also receive use of a Zil or a
Chaika (usually with a chauffeur), a free apartment
and dacha, and the right to shop in special stores.

An average salary is about 270 rubles per month.
That may not seem like a great deal of money, but rent,
utilities, and transportation cost much less than in
the West. Other items, particularly manufactured

goods and some foods, cost much more. A pair of shoes costs 50 rubles. A television set costs 400 rubles. One orange, imported from Morocco, costs 80 kopeks, if sold "on the street," half that much if purchased in a government grocery store. American jeans are very popular and sometimes sell for $100 U.S. on the illegal "black market." This is a system where individuals buy things from tourists and sell them secretly to others; if they are caught, they will spend time in prison.

Shopping

There are large department stores in the major cities, but no huge supermarkets or shopping malls. One of the largest department stores is found in Moscow and is named *GUM*. It's just across the street from the Kremlin, and its passageways are covered with domed skylights. It really isn't one big store, but a collection of small shops and stores all in one location. In a way it is a shopping mall, but without acres of parking spaces.

In these department stores you can buy clothes, shoes, cosmetics, or cameras and film. If you look carefully, you may even find a Pac Man machine in one of the corners!

But if you want to buy meat, you must go to a butcher shop. If you want bread, you go to a bakery. If you want vegetables or cheese, you must go to another specialty shop. In most cities, there is a city market where farmers sell some of their surplus products.

Soviet people spend a lot of time shopping for things. Here's what it's like to buy a candy bar: First you stay in line to tell the salesperson which candy bar you want, and to ask how much it costs. Then you go to a second line and wait until you reach the cashier, where you pay for your candy bar, for which you are given a receipt. Then you return to the first line, wait your turn, hand over your receipt and hope that your favorite candy bar is still available. Buying things requires standing in line—and a lot of patience.

Often supplies run out early in the day. People stand in line for bakeries to open, for example, so they can buy fresh bread while it lasts. When the bread is sold out, the bakery is closed for the rest of the day. Even children carry tiny string bags in their pockets, so they will have something in which to carry some last-minute purchase, perhaps oranges or even a fresh chicken sold from stands on street corners.

Food and Drink

Soviet families try to have at least one or two meals each day together. What do they drink and what do they eat?

Everyone in the family helps with grocery shopping. People often keep string bags handy for carrying home their purchases.

There is milk. There is *kvas*, a kind of non-alcoholic "root beer" made from dried-out rye bread and yeast. There is seltzer water (called "gassy water"!) which is sold in vending machines, as is at least one famous American soft drink (Pepsi). Vodka is strictly for adults and is a strong alcoholic drink made from potatoes.

But the main drink, for adults and children, is tea. It's usually brewed and served from a *samovar*. This is a brass urn, with a faucet or spigot, used to boil water. It has an inner cylinder into which hot charcoal is placed. A small teapot resting on top of the samovar contains triple-strong brewed tea. You pour some of that extra-strong tea into a cup or glass and add boiling water. Samovars are found almost everywhere, even in railroad cars!

The tea is usually served in glasses, but not as iced tea. The glasses are specially treated to hold hot liquids. A silver spoon is often placed inside the glass, which helps keep the glass from cracking. There are special holders for the glasses; some of them are made of silver. Sugar and lemon may be added, but Soviet people often stir in a couple of large spoonfuls of strawberry or some other fruit jam.

Soviet families eat lots of bread. They try to buy it while it's hot, just out of the oven. You can find healthful Russian bread such as Russian rye or Jewish rye

Bread is an important food item to Soviet people. Often people line up early in the morning to purchase freshly-baked loaves.

bread in most supermarkets and bakeries. Spread some butter and jam, or add a slice of cheese or meat.

Caviar is an appetizer. It's very salty and not everyone likes the taste. Actually, caviar is fish eggs, or roe, from either salmon or sturgeon. Another popular appetizer is herring. It may be smoked (something like

English kippers) or the herring fillets may be rolled and marinated in a tomato-oil or a sour cream sauce.

Salads are popular; sometimes they're even eaten at breakfast! There are shredded carrots, slices of radishes or cucumbers with sour cream, or a salad called *vinaigrette* (diced carrots, beets, and potatoes mixed in oil, herbs, and vinegar).

There are several hearty, favorite soups. A cabbage or sauerkraut soup, which, in Russian, is pronounced *shchyee*, is usually made from pork. It's hard to pronounce but it's good to eat. (Here's a hint on how to handle that "shch" sound, which is a separate letter in Russian: say the words "mar*sh ch*air" rapidly and then try to repeat the "shch" sound alone.) Then there are two kinds of *borscht*. One is a thick vegetable soup which includes cabbage. The other is a beet soup, which is served either hot or cold with dabs of sour cream. Other hot soups include barley and mushroom, chicken broth with meat dumplings, and a thick fish soup called *solyanka ribnaya*. Cold soups are popular, too. In addition to cold beet borscht, there are fruit soups and a cold meat soup cooked in kvas, the drink made from rye bread.

Many families make an entire meal of these filling soups. But there is more to come at dinnertime, and especially when guests have been invited. A main dish will include meat and vegetables. The meat might be a "cutlet," which could be a veal or a pork chop, or just a large hamburger patty. *Shashlik* is pieces of lamb grilled on skewers like shishkebobs. There are spicy *goulashes* (stews) and peppery sausages. *Beef stroganoff*, sauteed cubes of beef or small meatballs cooked in a sour cream sauce, is often served with noodles. If you prefer something other than meat, you can choose from chicken (*chicken Kiev*, boned chicken breast stuffed with butter and cheese, is delicious), duck, or some sort of fish. Sturgeon, pike, perch, and halibut are popular. There is also a large catfish called a sheatfish which is sometimes available.

Potatoes are usually part of every meal. They are not only boiled or mashed but also served as pancakes and as a potato cake called *kugel*. In pancakes or kugel, potatoes are grated and mixed with some flour and an egg or two. Pieces of onion and bacon are added, and then the mixture is fried or baked. The "cake" is cut into squares when served.

Potatoes are also made into dumplings and filled with cottage cheese or meat. A dough is made of mashed and freshly grated potatoes. The dough is folded over the stuffing and boiled. Some of these dumplings are shaped like blimps (they're even called "zeppelins"). Melted butter is poured over them, or they are served with sour cream. Potato pancakes and kugel are also served with sour cream.

In Eastern Europe, as well as in the Soviet Union, cabbage is a popular vegetable. It is eaten boiled by itself or included in soups and stews.

Well, what's for dessert?

Piroshki, a kind of fritter, are popular. So are very thin pancakes filled with jam, called *blinki*. Rice pudding is a favorite, covered with a thickened fruit topping. There is plenty of fresh fruit. And ice cream, called *marozhinaya*, is plentiful.

Perhaps you'd like to prepare a Russian meal.

Beet Borscht Soup

3 bouillon cubes
4 cups boiling water
1 No. 2 can of shoestring beets
1 green onion, finely chopped
1 small cucumber, diced
1 hard-boiled egg, chopped
1/2 pint sour cream or buttermilk

1. Dissolve the bouillon cubes in boiling water. Add the can of beets. Cool this for 15 minutes.

2. Add the finely cut green onion, the diced cucumber, and the chopped egg. Blend in the sour cream or buttermilk.

3. Chill for several hours.

Borscht can be served with hot boiled potatoes. It's a great meal for a hot day.

When they have company over for dinner, many people go "all out" and fix a large meal. They might serve the cutlets below with a delicious potato dish, such as potato kugel.

Hamburger "Cutlets" with Sauce

6 hamburger patties
1 slice of white, day-old bread
1/4 cup horseradish
1 pint sour cream or plain yogurt
A blender

1. Start the hamburgers cooking. You could fry, broil, or barbecue them. You will make the sauce while they cook.

2. Tear up the bread into small pieces and put it in the blender. Add the horseradish and the sour cream or yogurt. Mix until smooth.

3. Put the sauce in a saucepan and simmer it on low heat until hot. When the hamburgers are done, top them with the hot sauce.

Kugel

4 cups of potatoes, peeled and cut into cubes
3 eggs
1 large onion, cut into four pieces
1 teaspoon salt
1/4 teaspoon pepper
1/4 cup melted margarine
1/3 cup all-purpose flour
1/2 cup crisp-fried bacon bits (optional)
Some fresh parsley
A blender
A strainer or colander

1. Heat the oven to 350 degrees. Grease a 1-1/2 quart casserole dish.

2. Put the cut-up potatoes in the blender and cover them with cold water. Chop them finely. Pour the contents of the blender into a fine-mesh strainer, or put paper towels into a colander and drain the potatoes that way. You don't want the water; you want the finely ground potatoes.

3. Put the drained potatoes back in the blender. Add the eggs, onion, salt, pepper, margarine, flour, and parsley, as well as the bacon if you're going to use

it. Mix all these ingredients until the parsley is chopped.

4. Pour the mixture into the greased casserole pan and bake it for an hour, or until it is brown. Cut it into squares and serve it hot.

Kugel is good with sour cream, but if you're getting tired of sour cream (or putting on weight from too many calories!) try applesauce with it.

Be careful, and good eating!

7. *The Twelve-Hour School Day*

We have said that the Soviet system of government is a planned economy. Education is also carefully planned, from earliest childhood through a graduate's first job.

Babies can be taken to nurseries as early as three months of age. Those nurseries are combined with kindergarten. Pre-school learning activities begin at about the age of three years. Thus, a child's education can begin very early—but the decision rests with the family, usually the mother.

Most mothers work. They are given a paid leave of two months before the birth of a child, and usually two months after that birth. (This leave may be even longer if she gives birth to twins, or if there were any problems with the birth.) The mother may take off another year after this, during which she will receive only a part of her regular salary. She may choose to take yet another year away from her job, but during this second year she will get no pay. After that second year, the mother must decide whether she will continue to look after her child herself, find help at home, or place her child in a day nursery. Sometimes a grandmother (called a *babushka*) can take care of the child. Although infants can be placed in nurseries as early as three months, very few

Soviet mothers choose to do so; only five babies out of every hundred begin their education so soon in life.

When the mother returns to work, if her child's day nursery is located near her factory or office, she is given time off to visit her baby during the day. Every three-and-a-half hours she may stay with her baby for thirty minutes.

Staying at home is no longer a choice once a child becomes six years old. Everyone must then attend a government school.

The Education System

Until recently, schooling was limited to ten years and began when a child turned seven. Since 1984, first grade begins at age six, and school continues for eleven years. Primary grades are one through three, middle level from grades four through eight, and secondary (or high school) education is from grades nine through eleven. There is no "senior year" in the Soviet system.

Afterward, students who continue their education in a technical school obtain a technician certificate with two more years of study. At a university, an engineer or a doctor will have to continue studies for another six years. Other university students get their degrees after five or six years, depending upon their area of study.

Classes are held six days a week. (Sundays are

The years of education required of Soviet students varies. For people who might like laboratory work, the requirement could be two years beyond secondary school.

free.) Classes continue for ten months, with vacation months being July and August. School begins at 7 a.m., and the school is open until 7 p.m., although classes usually end by 3 p.m. The extra time in the afternoon is used for projects, club activities, sports, cleanup chores, and study hall. This twelve-hour school day provides activities and security for children whose parents must work. By the way, as many as four hot meals are served each day to school children.

While students wear uniform-like clothing in school, they dress as they please away from the classroom.

Obeying the Rules

Students are required to wear uniform-like clothes to school. The girls usually wear a black or a white smock over their regular dress. The boys wear suits, usually gray or brown, with white shirts (but no ties). Of course, they wear what they wish when they are away from school.

Students are expected to keep their classrooms and playground clean. At least two hours a week are spent in cleanup in the school. High school students work an extra afternoon each week in the parks or the neighborhood. Soviet students take pride in how they look and how their school and town look.

Discipline can be very strict. Lots of homework is assigned and if someone doesn't turn it in on time, or if his or her grades fall, his or her name is sent to the factory or office where the student's parents work. The names are posted on the bulletin boards.

Monitors are appointed in each class. They are chosen from the students, and this selection is considered to be a high honor. A monitor records attendance and helps the teacher keep order. Each morning in Soviet schools, monitors read a list of students who misbehaved the previous day.

There are parent-teacher meetings, something like our PTA, but with a big difference. Conferences with parents are not private but are part of a public meeting. A student's difficulties are described, and sometimes the parents are blamed for their children's poor performance or behavior.

School Subjects

Education is taken very seriously. There is a great deal of emphasis upon mathematics and science, and the Soviet educational system has produced many excellent mathematicians and scientists.

Soviet students are proud of the way their schools look. They help keep schoolyards clean with small brooms like the one this girl holds, and help clean up their towns as well.

Of course, schools in smaller towns do not have the same equipment as city schools. Also, not every student is able to keep up with the required subjects; even so, there is lots of pressure on both students and teachers for students to get and maintain good grades. Teachers are themselves "graded" on how many students pass each year.

In those Soviet republics where Russian is not the native language (as in Armenia or Estonia, for example), Russian must be learned beginning in the fourth grade. Learning Russian is important if a student wishes to attend a university. Another foreign language may also be studied starting in fourth grade; many students choose English.

During the eleven years of schooling that all students get, everyone studies just about the same material. There are no independent school districts, as we have. The school subjects and the textbooks are chosen in Moscow for the whole country.

More than just languages, science, and mathematics is taught in class. There is discussion of politics and there is *propaganda.* Propaganda is information that builds up one group's or person's reputation while tearing down other groups or people. A law states that "the school should ally the Marxist-Leninist conception [idea] of the world" with patriotism and respect for past traditions.

This system of education also provides specialists the Soviet Union requires. Since skilled workers are needed in factories, a certain number of young people must complete studies at trade or technical schools. Since interpreters are needed in the diplomatic corps or as guides for foreign visitors, other gifted students study at the foreign language institutes.

As in schools everywhere, Soviet children are expected to be cooperative in class. The children wearing red hats are monitors; they help teachers check attendance and keep order.

Communism is taught and encouraged. Even in a first-grade classroom you will find a *Lenin Corner.* This almost looks like a shrine; a picture of V.I. Lenin, the first leader of the Soviet Union, is in it. The picture is decorated with ribbons, and there may be a vase filled with flowers. Underneath is a shelf with some of Lenin's books on it.

After-School Groups

After-school youth organizations have strong ties to politics, as well. Very young children can join the *Little Octobrists*, named after the Great October Revolution. This club is for children aged seven to nine. When a child is ten, he or she may join the *Young Pioneers*. Pioneers add a bright red handkerchief to their school uniform. A student remains a Pioneer until age fourteen.

Octobrists and Pioneers have been compared to the two age levels of scouting. There is some similarity. Children participate in public service work, recreation, and camping. They develop skills and a concern for ecology. But there is also some military and much political instruction. Pioneers become good with a rifle. They appear in many parades, which are often shared with the military. There is much emphasis upon defending "Mother Russia" and having respect for the Party and its decisions. Obedience to leaders is stressed. There is much study of socialism, Communism, and atheism.

Atheism is the belief that there is no God. It may seem strange that atheism is taught. There are schools that prepare instructors to attack religion and encourage atheism. These instructors speak at union meetings in factories and farms, at school assemblies, and to

Science is one of the subjects most emphasized in Soviet schools. These children are attending astronomy classes in Moscow's Palace of Culture.

youth organizations. Every large city has an Atheism Museum to which children are taken on field trips. These museums have displays that make fun of religious life and institutions. A recent school poster shows a cosmonaut waving from his spaceship, shouting "There is no God." Below him, the poster shows church steeples falling down.

At age fifteen, a student is old enough to join the *Komsomol*. This is the *Young Communist League*.

This group is clearly political in its activities. You must first be a Komsomol member if you ever wish to become a member of the Communist Party. You cannot become a Komsomol member unless you are recommended by a member of the Party and two members of the Komsomol. Being a member of this group may be the only way to gain admission to a university.

A person is not forced to join any of these groups. However, there is a lot of what is known as peer pressure. If you don't join the Pioneers, for example, you won't have a red handkerchief to wear to class. When you are the only person not wearing a red handkerchief in the class, you are obviously not one of the crowd. Teachers may suggest that you reconsider. Your fellow students might beg you to join. That's peer pressure. If parents object too strongly to that pressure, they can have their parental rights taken away. Their children could be sent off to a boarding school, perhaps in another city, and be raised by the State.

Problems in Planned Education

There are no private nor religious schools in the Soviet Union. Even Sabbath schools and Sunday schools are not allowed. The Soviet constitution states that not only must there be separation of church and state but also separation of church and school. This presents a difficult problem for parents who practice a religion. Some feel that they can balance the official instruction in Communism and atheism by teaching their values at home. Other parents fear the results of that official instruction, and will organize underground (illegal) church or synagogue schools, and risk arrest. The rigid educational system in the Soviet Union is a reason many parents give for wanting to emigrate to some other country.

Nevertheless, aside from its politics and propaganda, Soviet education is thorough and skillful. To be sure, the better schools are in the big cities. But even in smaller towns where staff and facilities are limited, students can better their education through study by mail. Sometimes they may travel to a larger center for night classes.

There are only about forty major universities in the Soviet Union, although there are dozens of technical institutes. Far more young people apply for admission to such institutions of higher learning than can be accepted. The entrance examinations are difficult, and competition is tough. Preferred universities are the Bauman School of Engineering in Moscow, the Moscow Foreign Language Institute, the Moscow Institute of Dramatic Art, and the Leningrad Law Faculty. Sometimes there are as many as a hundred applicants for a single opening. Once someone is accepted by a university, and after he or she has completed a course of study, that student must agree to go wherever the government sends him or her on that person's first job. But students do have a guarantee of a first job. That is also part of the Soviet planned economy.

Perhaps it is only fair that students owe something to the government. All education in the Soviet Union is free. In fact, university and technical students who get good grades get a living allowance.

Free public education in Russia began just before the turn of this century. Leo Tolstoy, the writer, was one of the first educators to experiment with free schooling, even among children of former serfs. There were private, religious schools, of course, run by churches or synagogues, and available only to wealthy people. Among the poor, fathers passed on what knowledge they had, but only to their sons. As this century began, only three Russians out of ten could read and write.

Times have changed. Except for a very few tribal languages which have not yet been put in written form, illiteracy has been abolished. That means that every adult can now read and write. For all of its citizens, education in the Soviet Union is required, available to everyone, and free.

8. Champions of Sports

Sport is the closest thing to a national religion in the Soviet Union. One in four persons participates in some kind of sport. It is so important that a government department rates people in their sport. Through their sports clubs, forty million people have obtained the status of *GTO*, which means they are "physically fit for work and defense." Seventy thousand persons have the rank of Master of Sports. Lenin set an example: every day he rode a bicycle and played chess (chess is considered a sport in the Soviet Union).

People are encouraged to be active in many ways. Sports "palaces" have been built in every major city, and these are well-equipped, beautiful places for conditioning and perfecting the body. A few large former churches have been made into gymnasiums. August 12 is National Physical Culture Day. And People's Games are an annual event, becoming a kind of mini-Olympics.

Children and Sports

Physical fitness training begins in the first grade. Six-year-olds have daily workouts, simple exercises and gymnastics. Since most schools do not have large athletic facilities, the Soviet Union has established special sports schools, especially in the larger cities. The Russian initials for these schools form the word *DIUSH*. Most people call them "schools without desks."

Anyone who is eleven years old, and shows some special talent for a sport, is encouraged to attend one of these sports schools. You must still attend your regular school, take all of your regular classes, and maintain high grades. Classes in sports are held in the afternoon and evening, after the regular school classes. Beginner classes are for youngsters from eleven to thirteen years of age, which meet for two hours three times a week. Later, the classes are increased to five days a week. You may continue in the sports school program until you are eighteen.

Each sports school does not offer everything; it specializes in three or four activities. A school might combine track, wrestling, and hockey, for example. Moscow has ten such schools, specializing in swimming, acrobatic gymnastics, volleyball, and chess. Kiev has seven schools. One of its schools concentrates on basketball, soccer, tennis, and ping-pong. That one school has three thousand students and sixty coaches. Each coach has a Physical Education degree and a Master of Sports rating.

Everyone, including children, is encouraged to become interested in sports and physical fitness.

Champions Everywhere

If a student is especially good in a chosen sport, his or her coach will recommend that the student concentrate on the sport at a higher-level sports school. There are also summer-long sports camps to which promising athletes are invited, with all expenses paid by the government. The Soviet Union likes to produce champions, and this is one way to do that.

The government encourages excellence in athletics by its rigid system of ranking. The highest rank is Honored Master of Sport, followed by Master of Sport—International Class and Master ranks, in Class A, Class B, and so on. The ranking is done by the ministries of culture and sport.

The Soviet Union did not participate in the Olympic Games until 1952, in Helsinki. It had boycotted the Olympics six times, from 1920 to 1948. But its athletes quickly made up for lost time. Soviet athletes won the greatest number of medals at the Games in Melbourne in 1956. They also led all other nations in medals in the 1972 Olympics in Munich, in 1976 in Montreal, and in 1980 in Moscow. (The 1980 Summer Olympics, held in Moscow, were boycotted by sixty-two nations, including the United States, as a protest against the Soviet invasion of Afghanistan. The Soviet Union, joined by fourteen other nations, boycotted the 1984 Summer Olympics in Los Angeles.) The total number of medals received thus far by Soviet athletes is 402 gold medals, 330 silver medals, and 296 bronze medals. It is an impressive record.

Soviet Olympians have excelled in gymnastics and track.

Male gymnastic champions have included Grant Shaginyan and Albert Azarian, both Armenians. Women gymnasts have won many medals. Among

Soviet athletes are world's champions in many sports. Olga Korbut was world-famous for her performances in the 1972 Olympics, where she took a gold medal in gymnastics.

them are Ludmilla Turscheva and tiny Olga Korbut. The gymnasts perform as a team and as individuals. In addition to the required events on balance beam, high bar, rings, parallel bars, and the vault, there are floor exercises and artistic gymnastics which have the feel of ballet.

Soviet women have set more track records than men. Tatiana Kazankina is an outstanding champion in both the 800 and 1500 meter races. Soviet men are excellent in such field events as the hammer throw, shot put, and triple jumps. They are medalists in weight lifting and wrestling. Alexander Medved is a champion wrestler.

Soviet women and men both excel in winter sports events, for which they have claimed many Olympic medals, particularly in ice skating and cross-country skiing. It was considered a major upset when the U.S. hockey team beat the Soviet champions at the Lake Placid Olympics in 1980; the Soviets had won the gold medal in hockey in 1964, 1968, 1972, and 1976.

Soviet athletes have been criticized in the West for being more professional than amateur. Professional athletes are paid for their sport, amateurs are not. The Soviet government responds by saying that none of its athletes receives a salary, and thus isn't a professional. Critics point out that champion athletes in the Soviet Union enjoy many privileges not available to the average citizen. They have special housing and food, and exceptional coaching and training. Their work schedules are adjusted so that there is plenty of time for practice—while they are paid for their "assigned work."

Mental Sport

The three most popular sports in the Soviet Union are soccer, hockey, and chess—in that order. You may find it hard to accept chess as a sport, but the Soviet people support it because they say it exercises the brain! Chess is a very old game, coming to Europe by way of India and Persia in the sixth century, some twelve hundred years ago. Played on a board that looks like a checkerboard, it's a military strategy game, played with a variety of pieces: castles, knights, bishops, pawns (foot soldiers), a queen, and a king. The players try to isolate each other's king so he cannot escape. That's called check-mate. The name for chess in Russian is *shach-mat*, which sounds a bit like "check-mate." "Check" or "shach" may come from the Persian (or Iranian) word *Shah*, which means "king."

International chess competition began in 1851. Alexander Alekhine was the first Russian to win the world chess championship. He held it from 1927 to 1935, although by this time he had left the Soviet Union. The Soviets claimed the championship again with Mikhail Botvinnik, who held the title from 1948 to 1957. Soviet chess players kept the title for twenty-four years, until an American, Bobby Fischer, won the title from Boris Spassky in 1972. Anatoli Karpov regained the title for the Soviet Union in 1975.

Instruction in chess is available to pre-schoolers. They use chess pieces that are almost as large as the children themselves, playing on a giant chess board on the floor! More serious study of chess begins in the fifth grade where students must learn the plays (gambits) of famous champions. There are frequent competitions in which both boys and girls participate. There are many after-school chess schools, with as many as three

Chess is a popular sport in the Soviet Union, where young and old alike play in national tournaments for rankings as well as for fun.

hundred children enrolled in a single school. The most famous chess schools are located in Leningrad and Moscow.

The highest ranking in chess is Grand Master, a person who has won major tournaments. A Master is a chess player who is eligible to play in restricted competition. Eligibility standards are determined by the International Chess Federation. Four thousand Soviet children have achieved the Master rank in chess!

Indoors or Outdoors

People joke that chess is popular in the Soviet Union because its winters are so long that there isn't anything else to do. That isn't quite true. Bad weather does not restrict sports activities. Some winter sports are just as popular as those of summer.

Soviet children love to ice skate, ski cross country, play ice hockey, and go sledding. A special sled is used, something like a *luge*, which you may have seen on television in the Winter Olympics. This sled is narrow, designed for one or two persons, and has high metal runners which are kept razor-sharp. Riders use their feet for steering.

Because of those long, cold winters, swimming has developed more slowly as a national sport—but the Soviets are changing that. More indoor pools are being built. Moscow has a huge outdoor swimming pool which is heated even during the coldest months.

However, the number one sport is soccer. Every large city has its own team; some cities have more than one "major-league" team. There are 100,000 soccer fields in the Soviet Union. Soccer in most of the non-English-speaking world is called football (sometimes spelled "futbol"). It's not a bad name because only the feet (and sometimes the head) are used to move the ball. Hands are never used, except by the goalie.

Another game played seriously and well in the Soviet Union is hockey. The best players often represent their country in the Olympic games, as these players did in 1980.

Another extremely popular Soviet sport is ice hockey. Hockey is a fast-paced game, played on an ice rink that looks something like a soccer field. The players use a hockey stick to move or hit a three-inch-wide rubber puck. There are goals with nets at either end, and a team scores one point each time the puck gets past the goalie who is guarding the net. There are six players on each team, and the game is played in three periods of twenty minutes each. Of course, each player and the referees wear ice skates. Ice hockey was invented in Canada and has been an Olympic sport since 1920. There are no "professional" hockey teams in the Soviet Union; however, some Soviet teams have played North

American professional teams in exhibition matches, and have shown their skills again and again.

Several other popular Soviet team sports have been imported from North America. Basketball was invented in 1891 by Dr. James Naismith, the physical director of the YMCA College in Springfield, Massachusetts. Originally, it was a game intended to be played indoors, in any weather. Today, basketball is popular all over the world. It is taught in Soviet sports schools and its coaches have developed special exercises to strengthen arms and hands.

Volleyball also has YMCA and Massachusetts origins, first played in 1895. It became very popular with American firemen, who appreciated the exercise and the short fifteen-point game. Since 1964 volleyball has been an Olympic event and is very popular in the Soviet Union, especially in the southern parts of the country where it can be played year-round.

Baseball, invented by Abner Doubleday in Cooperstown, New York, in 1839, is a new sport in the Soviet Union. It was introduced there by Cuban students. Soviet children have long played a game they call *lapta*, which is a close cousin to baseball.

Soviet children have found many ways to use open fields or parks or even backyards for their games. The large sports palaces and arenas are not found everywhere. And so the children play *mini-football*, played like soccer, but on a smaller field and with simplified rules. They have a kind of wrestling and judo called *Sambo*. It's for boys only and it's described as "self defense without weapons."

Magazines published for school children include ideas and instructions for many games. Local soccer teams form "leather ball" clubs. There are "golden puck" clubs for young hockey players. Another favorite activity is the "Auto-Scooter Racers' Club." Children build vehicles similar to soapbox derby racers. Doing this, they learn the basics of auto mechanics and the requirements for a drivers' license.

Why is there so much interest in sports in the Soviet Union?

Healthy trained bodies are a national resource, of course. Cross-country skiing ability was important when the Soviet Union fought Finland in 1940. Marksmanship with guns is more than a sport. So is parachute-jumping, which is a "sport" in some parts of the Soviet Union.

But healthy bodies also mean healthy students and workers. The Soviet people believe that fresh air, fresh water, and lots of exercise are essential to health and personal well being. Obviously, the Soviet leaders agree, and provide a large-scale program thoughout the country. It is practical in a planned economy to have people who are competitive, achieving, mentally alert, and physically fit.

Whatever the reasons, the Soviet people are committed to excellence in physical sports and performance. It is wonderful to see the majority of people in a country participate in sports, rather than just watch.

9. *Russian Flowers in American Soil*

Each time you look at a Lincoln penny, you see a reminder of a Russian immigrant to the United States. His name was Victor David Brenner, and he was a sculptor. Brenner was born in 1871 in Lithuania, which was then part of the Russian empire. He came to the United States in 1890. In 1909, he was asked to design a coin that would celebrate the one hundredth birthday of Abraham Lincoln. This was the first U.S. coin that honored a single person. Although the design was slightly changed in 1959, the Lincoln penny remains very much as Brenner designed it.

Slavic and Baltic immigrants arrived much earlier than Victor Brenner. There was a Ukrainian among the 105 settlers who founded Jamestown in 1607. We don't know if he was among the thirty-two survivors of the first year, in which two-thirds of the original settlers died, but the name of Lavrenty (Lawrence) Bohun appears on Captain John Smith's list of pioneer residents.

The first Russian immigrant to the American colonies was Charles Thiel. He was born in St. Petersburg, was trained in medicine and pharmacy, but somehow displeased Empress Catherine the Great. Thiel escaped to Philadelphia in 1769, seven years before the colonies declared their independence. He changed his last name to Cist, and changed his profession as well. First, he became a printer and a publisher. One of his books was Thomas Paine's *The American Crisis.* Later, Cist became an explorer and discovered anthracite, an extremely hard and long-burning coal that was an excellent fuel. He started the Lehigh Coal Mining Company in Pennsylvania. His descendants became leaders in sociology, science, and the armed forces.

At one time, Russia owned the land that is now Alaska. In 1799, Russian settlers established a village there. It was first called New Archangel, but was renamed Sitka. The Russians built other outposts for their fur-trading business, even building two forts in northern California. The United States purchased Alaska from Russia in 1867, paying seven million dollars.

An interesting immigrant-settler from Russia was Ivan Veniaminov. He was a missionary who came with his family to Alaska. He became an expert in the Indian Aleut language. In fact, he compiled a dictionary, a grammar book, and a simple "first reader" in the Aleut language. Veniaminov translated parts of the Bible, became Alaska's first bishop, and built St. Michael's Cathedral in Sitka (which is still standing). He was called back to Russia, but during his ten years in Alaska he established thirty-six churches. In Russia, he was named Metropolitan of Moscow, which is a high position in the Russian Orthodox Church.

There are descendants of these early settlers living in Alaska and on the West Coast. The Russian Orthodox Church continues to be active in North America. Its headquarters are now located in New York City, but about 150 churches are scattered throughout Canada and the United States, with more than 200,000 members.

Rich and Poor

During the last century, life in Russia was hard and cruel. The peasants (serfs) had been treated as slaves and were given their freedom only in 1861. They were too poor to leave the estates on which they had worked for so long. During this time, the only Russians who came to North America were such people as Charles Thiel. These were wealthy persons, often with close ties to the court, who were in disfavor with the czar and often had to flee for their lives.

By the early 1900s, some of those former serfs, or children of serfs, scraped and saved enough money to pay the $100 it took to cross the Atlantic Ocean. Hundreds of them had decided that they wanted a new home with the hope of a better future.

They were poor people. In Russia, if they were

workers, they had worked twelve hours a day in unsafe factories. If they were farmers, they often worked even longer in the fields. They could not save any money. Their children could not get an education. There was no constitution, and they had no rights. Some chose not to fight for the czar in his war against the Japanese.

They had a dream that things would soon be better for them in the United States. They found that it would not be an easy time for them. They did not speak English, and the only jobs they could find were in coal mines or steel mills or stockyards, where they could live close to other Russian immigrants and speak their own language. A very few lucky immigrants found farms on which they could work, and later buy. Many Ukrainians went to western Canada where they were given homesteads. If they cleared the land, built a shelter, began to farm, and stayed for seven years, the homestead of 360 acres would be theirs.

It was a difficult time for many of these peasant immigrants. Since they kept to themselves, speaking their own language, they ran into much suspicion and discrimination from others. Many Eastern European workers joined labor unions; some were radical in their political views and were called Communists. A few probably were Communists, but certainly not all of the immigrant workers.

During World War I, Russia made a separate

peace with Germany after the Russian revolution of 1917. In many places, Russian immigrants were called traitors. Following that revolution, a few of these immigrants wanted to return to their homeland, now called the Soviet Union. They knew how bad things had been under the czar; this is why they had left to look for freedom in another land. They believed that conditions would be better in their homeland, and they were homesick. But they could not get passports. The United States did not establish diplomatic ties with the Soviet Union, which would allow travel between the two countries, until 1933.

Religious Immigrants

Since 1820, when the Bureau of the Census began to keep immigration figures, nearly four million people came to the United States from lands that now make up the Soviet Union. Half of this number arrived during the twenty-year period between 1890 and 1910.

Many came for religious reasons, long before the Communists came into power. Some were German Mennonites who settled in Pennsylvania, Indiana, Kansas, and Canada. Originally they had moved from Holland and Prussia to the Ukraine at the invitation of Catherine the Great. The Mennonites were pacifists, believing that it was wrong for them ever to fight in a

At times it has been difficult for people of different religions to practice their faiths in the Soviet Union. Lutherans, Catholics, Jews, and even the Pentacostalist Christians above have left the country for this reason.

war, no matter what the circumstances. The Empress Catherine allowed them to live their peaceful lives, but by 1870 Czar Alexander II was stressing both Russian nationalism and military power. It was not a good time to be both German and a pacifist, and to live in Russia. And so these German Mennonites, who were now Russian citizens, went looking for a new home. Other Germans living in Russia, who were Catholics or Lutherans, also emigrated and settled in the Dakotas.

The Molokans were a religious group that split off from the Russian Orthodox Church. *Molokan* is a nickname, in Russian, for "milk drinkers." These people drank only milk during Lent, the forty-six-day period before Easter. Like the Mennonites, Molokans also refused to take human life. About five thousand Molokans emigrated to the United States between 1905 and 1907. They settled in California, mostly in the Los Angeles area. Their little colony became known as "Russian Town."

Another religious immigrant group was the Dukhobors. These people totally rejected the official Russian church and as a result were severely harassed. They had no priests. They were vegetarians and lived simple lives as farmers. Many of them settled in western Canada.

Russian Jews began their trek to the New World in the late 1880s. Jews were killed or crippled in the *pogroms*, a Russian word that means "devastation." They were allowed to live only in an area called the "Pale of Settlement." They were forbidden to go "beyond the Pale," which extended from the Polish border to the Dnieper River and from the Baltic to the Black Sea. Life became dreadful, though under Catherine the Great they were allowed to have their own schools, where Yiddish and Hebrew were taught and spoken.

That also changed with the new policies of the czar. It became law that the only language that could be taught and spoken was Russian. This immediately became a problem for the Jews, as well as others. It affected Germans who had not yet left. This rule affected Estonians, Latvians, and Lithuanians whose languages are not Slavic, and who write in the Roman alphabet, not the Russian Cyrillic alphabet. This new Russian nationalism produced thousands of emigrants.

World War II brought a new wave of immigrants from Eastern Europe. During the war, thousands of Soviet citizens were captured by the Nazis. Most of the Soviet Jews were sent to extermination camps. Other Soviet citizens became "labor slaves" and were sent back to Germany to work on farms or in factories. After the defeat of Adolf Hitler, many of these Soviet people decided to remain in the West. They were called *DPs*—displaced persons—and thousands of them were granted citizenship and new homes in the United States and Canada.

The immigration continues today, but on a much smaller scale. Today, it is difficult to obtain an exit visa from the Soviet Union. To do so, you must give up your Soviet citizenship in advance. Without citizenship, you no longer have a job. Worse yet, you don't know for sure if you will be allowed to leave. Only fifty thousand Soviet citizens were allowed to emigrate to the United States within the past ten years.

A few still come for religious reasons. George Vins, a Baptist pastor who had been jailed, was permitted to leave in exchange for a Soviet spy. Two Pentecostal families who lived nearly five years in the basement of the U.S. embassy in Moscow were finally given exit visas.

Others of these new arrivals are intellectuals and dissidents. They dissent or disagree with Soviet policies, and they have chosen to seek freedom in the West. They do not emigrate as often as they defect or are sometimes exchanged for Russian citizens being held in the West.

Famous Citizens

The Western world has benefitted greatly from these talented people. Here are names of a few people who came to the United States and Canada during the 1900s, who have enriched life for all of us:

Vladimir Zworykin is called the "father of television." He invented the iconoscope, the camera tube that makes television possible. Igor Sikorsky is an aviation pioneer, best known as the inventor and designer of helicopters. George Gamow is an atomic scientist, who worked on the theory of nuclear fission. A crater on the moon has been named for him.

Among writers who have adopted the West are Vladimir Nabokov and Sholom Aleichim. Aleichim wrote about Jewish life in Russia and one of his stories

Many talented people from the Soviet Union now practice their arts in the United States. Conductor Mstislav Rostropovich is with the National Symphony in Washington, D.C.

is the basis for the musical *Fiddler on the Roof.* Other writers include Alexander Solzhenitsyn and Dr. Isaac Asimov. Asimov has written dozens of books but may be best known for his science fiction. He was born in Russia, brought to this country as a child, and is now a naturalized American citizen.

Many famous musicians have come: Igor Stravinsky, the composer; Sergei Rachmaninoff, the pianist; Yascha Heifetz, Vladimir Horowitz, Yehudi Menuhin, and Isaac Stern, all violinists; Serge Koussevitsky, the former conductor of the Boston Symphony; and Dmitri Tiomkin, a frequent winner of Academy Awards for his movie scores. Sol Hurok, a producer of concerts, is a Russian-American. So is the songwriter, Irving Berlin. Among the most recent musical newcomers is Mstislav Rostropovich, a cellist who now conducts the National Symphony in Washington, D.C. He won the Lenin Prize for music in 1964. Another is Maxim Shostakovich, the son of the famous composer.

A Russian dancer who has graced Western stages is George Balanchine. He will be remembered as the creator of modern American ballet. Rudolf Nureyev defected several years ago, joined later by Mikhail Baryshnikov and Alexander Godunov. All three are spectacular ballet dancers.

Of all the recent immigrants from the Soviet Union, Svetlana Allilueva was one of the most interesting. More than anyone else, she was familiar with the workings of the Soviet Union. She grew up in the Kremlin, because her father was Joseph Stalin, the former dictator of the country. During a visit to India in 1967, she took refuge in the U.S. embassy there and refused to return to the Soviet Union. Allilueva came

Svetlana Allilueva, daughter of Joseph Stalin, came to live in the West in 1967, but returned to the Soviet Union in 1984 with her U.S.-born daughter.

to the United States, married an American citizen, and chose to lead a quiet life. She started another family. She wrote books about her life and thoughts and went back to her church and her religious faith. She moved to Great Britain for a while, but in 1984 decided to return to the Soviet Union, taking her thirteen-year-old American-born daughter with her. Reports said that she was homesick and wished to see children and grandchildren from her first marriage in the Soviet Union. Some said that she became upset with the emphasis on money and possessions in the West.

Three million people have come to U.S. shores from the countries and areas that now make up the Soviet Union. They fondly remember their "Motherland." Sometimes these immigrants are homesick, too. But for the most part, these people prefer to live in the West, where they have the chance and the right to preserve what is their own: to speak their own language, practice their faiths, read newspapers freely published in their own languages, remember the past, and try to adjust to the future. Their children and grandchildren are rapidly becoming American. Together, they want to treasure their heritage and create new traditions, to live in peace with themselves and their neighbors.

Appendix A

Soviet Consulates, Embassies, and Travel Offices in the United States and Canada

Information from Soviet consulates can help Americans and Canadians understand Russian ways. Books and magazines, addresses of government offices and other organizations are available from them. Also listed are two Intourist offices. Intourist is the official Soviet travel agency. Your local travel agent will probably also have information about the Soviet Union.

U.S. Consulates, Embassy, and Travel Office

USSR Embassy
1125 16th St. NW
Washington, D.C. 20036
Telephone: (202) 628-7551

USSR Consulate General
2790 Green St.
San Francisco, CA 94123
Telephone: (415) 922-6642

USSR Consulate
1825 Phelps Pl. NW
Washington, D.C. 22008
Telephone: (202) 332-1483

Intourist
630 Fifth Ave., Suite 868
New York, NY 10111
Telephone: (212) 757-3884/5

Canadian Consulates and Travel Office

USSR Consulate General
3655 Avenue de Musee
Montreal, PQ H3G 2E11
Telephone: (514) 843-5901

USSR Consulate
52 Range Road
Ottawa, ON K1N 8JB
Telephone: (613) 236-7220

Intourist
1801 McGill College Ave.
Montreal, PQ 43A 2N4
Telephone: (514) 849-6394

Appendix B
The Russian Alphabet

Russian is the official language of the Soviet Union. Even though, like English, it is one of the Indo-European languages, it sounds quite different. The Russian words we use in the West are written to sound like Russian, even though there is no similarity in spelling.

Russian, like Polish or Czech, is a Slavic language. All Slavic languages developed from the languages the Slav tribes spoke early in Russia's history. But there are differences among these languages, especially in their alphabets. Polish and Czech, for example, use an alphabet almost identical to our alphabet, called the Roman alphabet. But Russian is written in the Cyrillic alphabet. The Cyrillic alphabet was based on the ancient Greek letters. Named after Saint Cyril, a ninth-century missionary, the Cyrillic alphabet is used in countries which accepted the Greek Orthodox ways of Christianity. The Roman alphabet came to be used in countries converted by missionaries of the Roman Catholic Church.

Below is a chart showing the Russian alphabet, as well as how the letters should be pronounced in Russian words.

Printed letter	Sounds like
А а	the *a* in car
Б б	the *b* in bar
В в	the *v* in vine
Г г	the *g* in good
Д д	the *d* in dog
Е е	*ye* as in yes
Ё ё	*yo* as in yonder
Ж ж	the *s* in treasure
З з	the *z* in zoo
И и	*ee* as in weed

Printed letter	Sounds like
Й й	*y* as in toy
К к	the *k* in kite
Л л	the *l* in lip
М м	the *m* in man
Н н	the *n* in no
О о	the *o* in or
П п	the *p* in pick
Р р	the *r* in ring
С с	the *s* in sad
Т т	the *t* in tiny
У у	*oo* as in good
Ф ф	the *f* in fill
Х х	the *h* in hot
Ц ц	*ts*, the *t* and the *s* sounds run together
Ч ч	the *ch* in chin
Ш ш	the *sh* in ship
Щ щ	*shyeh*, said very shortly
Ъ ъ	the hard sign (not pronounced by itself)
Ы ы	the *i* in pit
Ь ь	the soft sign (not pronounced by itself)
Э э	the *e* in let
Ю ю	*you*
Я я	*yah*

Glossary

Aeroflot (AIR·ah·flut)—official Soviet airline

Akademgorodok (ah·kah·DYEM·go·ro·dock)—
Siberian city

babushka (bah·BOOSH·kah)—grandmother

blinki (BLIN·kee)—pancakes

Bog (BAWGH)—God

bogatyr (BAWGH·ih·tahr)—knight-hero

Bolshevik (BOWL·sheh·vik)—member of the Communist majority

Bolshoi (BOWL·shoy)—the name of both a theater
and a ballet company in Moscow

borscht (BORSHT)—a soup, made either from beets
or from meat and vegetables

byliny (bee·LIN·ee)—songs or ballads

caviar (KAV·ee·ahr)—an appetizer spread made from
fish eggs

Chaika (CHY·kah)—small luxury car

Communism (KAHM·you·nizm)—a political theory
or system based on the ownership of all property
by the whole community. The Soviet Union is governed by the Communist Party but calls itself a
"socialist nation," in which every citizen shares in
work and production.

czar (ZAHR)—king or emperor

dacha (DACH·ah)—country or vacation home

Duma (DOO·mah)—the first Russian congress; today called the Supreme Soviet

Dyed Maroz (DYED mah·ROHZ)—Grandfather Frost, a Santa Claus-like figure

goulash (GOO·lahsh)—a meat stew

grozny (GROWZ·nee)—terrible; to be feared or dreaded

gulag (GOO·lahg)—a work camp for prisoners

GUM (GOOM)—the "State Universal Department Store," a collection of shops located on Red Square

intelligentsia (in·tell·uh·GENT·see·ah)—the educated, important, "upper" class of people in the Soviet Union

izba (IZ·bah)—farm house or log cabin

Khristos voskress (kris·TOS vohs·KRESS)—phrase meaning "Christ is risen"

Kiev (KEY·eff)—old city in the Soviet Union

Komsomol (KAWM·suh·mahl)—the Young Communist League

kopek (KOH·pek)—the smallest unit of Soviet money, like the cent in America

koulich (KOO·lich)—cake baked at Easter

krasnaya (KRAHS·nay·uh)—word meaning either "red" or "beautiful"

Kremlin (KREM·lin)—means "fortress"; where the central Soviet government has its offices

kugel (KOO·gel)—a potato, flour, and egg dish
kulak (KOO·lahk)—owner of a small farm
kvas (kuhVAS)—drink flavored by sour rye bread
marozhinaya (mah·ROHZ·zhin·ay·ya)—ice cream
Moscow (mosk·VAH)—capital of the Soviet Union
muzhiki (moo·ZHEE·kee)—peasants; members of the
    "lower" class of people in the Soviet Union
Novosibirsk (no·vo·see·BIRSK)—city in Siberia
Politburo (POH·lit·boo·roo)—fourteen-member
    committee with great power in the government
pogrom (poh·GRAHM)—violent attack on Jews
Pravda (PRAHV·duh)—means "truth"; the Com-
    munist Party newspaper
pysanky (pih·SAHNK·ee)—decorated eggs for Easter
ruble (ROO-bul)—the basic unit of money, like a
    dollar in America
samovar (sam·oh·VAR)—appliance used to make tea
shashlik (SHASH·lik)—grilled lamb on a skewer
shazki (SHAHZ·kee)—folk stories
shchyee (SHCHEE·yuh)—pork soup
solyanka ribnaya (sohl·YAHN·kah RIB·niy·uh)—fish
    soup
soviet (soh·vee·YET)—council
soyuz (soy·YUZ)—union or alliance
Voistinu voskress (VOY·stin·yu vos·KRESS)—
    phrase meaning "He is risen indeed"
Zil (ZILL)—expensive, luxury Soviet car

Selected Bibliography

Azbel, Mark Yakovlevitch. *Refusenik: Trapped in the Soviet Union.* Boston: Houghton Mifflin, 1981.

Bortoli, Georges. *Moscow and Leningrad Observed.* Trans. by Amanda and Edward Thomson. Oxford: Oxford University Press, 1975.

Cole, Ann, Carolyn Haas, Elizabeth Heller, and Betty Weinberger. *Children Are Children Are Children: An Activity Approach to Exploring.* New York: Little, Brown, and Co., 1978.

Eubank, Nancy. *The Russians in America.* Minneapolis: Lerner Publications, 1973.

The Europa Yearbook 1983. London: Europa Publications Ltd., 1983.

Jackson, W. A. Douglas. *Soviet Union.* Grand Rapids: The Fideler Co., 1980.

Kerblay, Basile. *Modern Soviet Society.* Trans. by Rupert Swyer. New York: Pantheon Books, 1983.

Lawrence, Sir John. *A History of Russia* (6th ed.). New York: New American Library, 1978.

Lee, Andrea. *Russian Journal.* New York: Vintage Books, 1984.

Manning, Clarence A. *The Forgotten Republics.* New York: Philosophical Library, 1952.

McDowell, Bart. *Journey Across Russia: The Soviet Today*. With photographs by Dean Conger. Washington, D.C.: National Geographic Society, 1977.

Morton, Miriam. *The Making of Champions: Soviet Sports for Children and Teenagers*. New York: Atheneum, 1974.

Paxton, John, ed. *The Statesman's Yearbook*. New York: St. Martin's Press, 1984.

Popescu, Julian. *Let's Visit the U.S.S.R.* (3rd ed.). London: Pegasus House, and Bridgeport, Connecticut: Burke Publishing Co., 1983.

Salisbury, Harrison E. *Moscow Journal* ("The End of Stalin"). Chicago: University of Chicago Press, 1961.

Shipler, David K. *Russia: Broken Idols, Solemn Dreams*. New York: Times Books, 1983.

Smith, Hedrick. *The Russians*. New York: Ballantine Books, 1976.

Snyder, Louis L. *The First Book of the Soviet Union*. New York: Franklin Watts, 1972.

Sternberg, Hilary, ed. *Fodor's Soviet Union*. New York: Fodor's Modern Guides, 1983.

Tripp, Rhoda Thomas, comp. *The International Thesaurus of Quotations*. New York: Thomas Y. Crowell, 1970.

The World Almanac and Book of Facts. New York: Newspaper Enterprises Association, 1984.

Index

About the Author

John Gillies has spent time in the Soviet Union twice in his life: as a child in Lithuania in the 1930s and as an adult in the 1980s. He brings "a child's memories and an adult's perceptions" to this overview of the Soviet Union. Through facts, honesty, and humor, Mr. Gillies hopes that an understanding of this giant land can be reached.

The author has worked in many fields. He has been a radio/television announcer, a missionary, and a communications consultant. His published works include a play, two novels, and, most recently, a guide to caring for parents as they age. *The Soviet Union* is his first book for children.

Mr. Gillies lives with his family in Austin, Texas.